Being responsible for hiring sales r[...] company is a really big job. The to[...] provide help me to be better at it. I[...] sales reps that know how to and aren't afraid to prospect. This assessment (BSRP's SPQ Gold® Sales Call Reluctance Report) measures exactly that.

Thanks guys for helping me look good!

—Terry Bean, Talent Magnet, Cavalier Telephone

With Minesh's invaluable help, I have been able to create accountability structure for my sales team. This has boosted our sales and sense of commitment to the company's goals.

—Johnna Goodwin, Changing Places Moving, MI

Managers: What You Don't Know can Hurt You

I am amazed after reading my Top Producer's DISC report and being coached on it that here is somebody I thought I knew very well for 6 years; the reality is that she is extremely stressed and in 'survival mode' which can hurt her and the team. She could have left the team. I am glad that now I can be effective in providing her the environment she needs!

—Jim Bass, Jim Bass Real Estate Group,
Real Estate Teams, LLC , MD

Minesh, Thanks for your expert execution at our Team Training Workshop. The 2 hour workshop was worth it for me in the first 10 minutes. I really think that you were able to quietly disarm each and every one in the room in order for them to feel comfortable to make some serious decisions to change.

I feel that everyone could use this in my office at least 1 time per year.

—Brendan Donelson, Access National Mortgage, TN

I feel like by using Minesh and Kim's services to do assessments on all my team members, it made it very clear as to which member should be performing which task. It is so important to have the right person, in the right seat on the bus doing the right job!

—Kendra Cooke, Crye-Leike's Middle
Tennessee's #1 Realtor,
2006 GNAR's Realtor of the Year

Your assistance in helping us evaluate new prospective sales people as well as support staff has been invaluable. We consistently refer back to the personality profile and work place motivators when ever a challenging situation arises or simply when we want to best reward someone for a job well done. Further, it is very advantageous for us to consult these reports when building new teams for our sister firm.

—*Barbara Vance, Prudential Florida WCI Realty, FL*

Your service has proven to be very accurate in assessing a new candidate's abilities. The reports generated also turn out to be essential to building a strong team and great management tools for those we hire. I would not hire again without using your services.

—*David Kammerer, Owner, Pacific Crest Home Loans, OR*

High achievers and entrepreneurs struggle to bring their team along. Minesh's ideas help me to lead and develop my team by becoming an effective communicator.

—*Scott Hardy, Flagstar Bank, VA*

It is really nice as a business owner to have a resource such as Minesh to know that his insight into the person your wanting to hire can save you as a business and a person a lot of time, energy and financial consideration by getting down to the "roots" of the person to know ahead whether you have a "weed" or a "rose garden". He certainly has saved me from some bad business decisions by his foresight into the people I am wanting to hire. He is great!!!!

—*Maria Wade-De La Cruz, Owner: Tuscan Residential & Investment Realty, LLC, TX*

Not only was the assessment test beneficial to hiring, I learned valuable information about myself in the process. Thank you Minesh!

—*Pam Hoepfl, Manager, Precision Funding, OR*

Minesh's services have been invaluable for our hiring process. As the Broker, it is vital that I hire personalities that energize the team dynamics, and bring on individual that have the same level of commitment to our clients. By understanding the mindset and tendencies of the potential hires, I am able to ask critical questions that result in a successful hire.

Thank you Minesh and Kim for providing an awesome service for our company.

—*Reeta Casey, VP / Broker, Stockworth Realty Group, FL*

Stop Hiring Losers

IDENTIFY WINNERS FOR YOUR TEAM WITH POWERFUL ASSESSMENTS

Minesh and Kim Baxi, CPBA, CPVA

Stop Hiring Losers:
Identifying Winners for Your Sales Team

Printed in the United States of America.

ISBN: **0-9790322-1-9**

Acknowledgements

We want to acknowledge four groups of people:

1. The CORE Training and Coaching Company and its leaders:
   Rick Ruby, Todd Scrima and Reeta Casey and their coaches.

2. Our clients who have given us the opportunity to assist them.

3. Our mentors in the Assessments business:
Bill Bonnstetter of Target Training International and its staff; Bill Brooks of The Brooks Group; Don and Lisa Lincoln of Focus: Forward Inc.; Winston and Barb Connor of Coaching Dynamics; George W. Dudley and Shannon L. Goodson, founders of Behavioral Sciences Research Press Inc's and their staff; Russell J. Watson, Ed.D. of Target Consultants, Inc.; Jennifer Zamecki of Well Run Concepts Inc.; and Stanley Mann of A Solution Coaching & Training, LLC.

4. The team who helped us complete the book project:
   Sally Rushmore, Dana Cadman, Norm Williams, Tressa Foster, Kathi Dunn and others.

Table of Contents

Chapter 1

Hire Slowly and Fire Quickly

Case History:
Real Estate Administrative Assistant

Drew Hendry, a successful real estate agent in Brentwood, Tennessee, had his mind set on one candidate. After spending numerous hours poring over resumes and interviewing candidates for the position of Administrative Assistant for his thriving real estate business, this candidate seemed the most fit for the job.

He decided to use our help in analyzing the candidate's suitability for the position. We administered our battery of assessments and came to the conclusion that this candidate might not be the best fit for the position.

Drew was in a quandary. This was the only candidate left. Should he hire or should he not?

He felt he had no choice and ended up hiring this person. Within 60 days we received his phone call to tell us that he had been forced to let this employee go. He told us that we had been right about the prognosis and he was convinced that he would never again hire without using our assessment tools and our guidance.

He began the search again. He was frustrated but more determined this time to find the right fit. After more interviews, he thought he had found a good fit. He resolved to have the assessments done on the new candidate. This time when the results came back, they showed that the person was a good fit. He was relieved but skeptical that there could be such a thing as a good fit. A good fit only goes so far.

The reports that came back also gave helpful advice and suggestions about how to motivate (and de-motivate) his right-hand person. Drew and his assistant reviewed how they could best work together. They go over these reports every 30 days. Using this method is building them into a strong cohesive team. Drew reports that he is thankful for his new assistant every day.

Is This Your Experience?

Have you been in such a situation where you were in a quandary as to which person would be the best candidate out of numerous applicants for the position? Certainly you do not want to be in the situation of hiring a person only to have to let him go in a short time.

A loan officer asked for our help in doing assessments on a prospective new employee. When we mentioned that the candidate was not suitable for the position, he disregarded our opinion. Just like Drew he soon reported that the employee did not work out.

We worked with him again and this time he brought us a candidate that did not seem to be a good fit either. We advised against hiring this candidate but he proceeded to hire her anyway. In a couple of months he was back complaining that this employee had not worked out either.

Having worked with hundreds of sales professionals and managers, we have identified common traits of people who fit the job descriptions. *The purpose of this short book is to assist you in making better hiring decisions.*

This book is not intended to be a detailed guide. We do not claim to be experts in the entire hiring process – we are not recruiters. Because the field of assessments is already vast and constantly evolving, we feel we cannot be jack-of-all-trades in hiring. Our field of expertise lies in using assessment tools to assist business owners and managers in identifying the candidate who is most likely to be productive in the assigned role and who fits most closely with the team profile.

We do suggest verbiage for ads, methods for attracting qualified candidates and ways to narrow the field of candidates using resumes, questionnaires and interviews. Kim is a qualified interviewer with a degree in Human Resource Development and she does offer great ideas for the interview process as well.

What you can expect to get from reading this book

Our purpose is three-fold:

1. First, we want to let you know that the hiring process is not something for which most professionals have any training. Even those who claim to be experts in hiring fail quite often to attract and keep the best talent. We shall devote a few pages to help you understand the cost of a bad hire.
2. Secondly, we will give you an overview of the hiring process and the steps you must take.
3. Lastly, we will give you templates of profiles based on our years of experience working with sales professionals and managers that we feel can make your hiring decision a lot easier. We have seen what works and what doesn't. We will share the assessment tools we use and we will give you the common traits for the positions for which you are likely to hire.

Cost Of A Bad Hire

Most managers like to make decisions quickly and might not feel that it is necessary to get help. You might be asking: is it really that expensive if you made a bad hire?

Let us evaluate what is the cost of a bad hire.

The accepted estimate for the cost of a bad hire is 1.5 to 3.5 times the salary of the job in question, after all costs are factored in. These costs can include, among other things:

+ Interview time
+ Reference checking time
+ Manager training time
+ Lost profit margins
+ Potential customer problems
+ Staff problems with low morale and/or having to replace an employee in the middle of an assignment

The Bureau of Labor Statistics estimates that it costs at least $14,000 to replace one employee.

Have you ever stopped to figure out exactly how much time you have to invest in hiring an employee? Activities like screening phone calls, reviewing resumes and arranging interviews can be very time-consuming.

By filling in the following "Hiring activities" chart, you will develop an accurate estimate of how much time you spend locating a suitable individual.

Hiring Activities	Hours Devoted
Developing position specifications *(job description, compensation package, etc.)*	
Writing, laying out and placing ad	
Screening phone calls (how many phone calls *might you receive to an ad?*)	
Receiving and scanning resumes *(how many resumes would you wade through to find a few good ones?)*	
Reviewing resumes *(what is the criteria?)*	
Developing a short list of possible candidates	
Arranging interviews *(how many first interviews would you need to schedule?)*	
Conducting first interviews *(Is there a script?)*	
Developing a second short list based on interviews	
Arranging second interviews	
Conducting reference checks	
Extending an offer	
Sending rejection letters	
Other recruiting and hiring activities	

Apart from the traditional costs of a bad hire, which include recruiting costs, training investments, and supervisory coaching time, a bad hire in a customer contact job will have a direct impact on customer retention. **Customers who are ill-treated leave and go to your competition.**

This estimate of the real cost of a bad hire doesn't even take into account costs which are extremely difficult to calculate, such as:

- The negative effect on co-workers' productivity and morale.
- Lost business and opportunities due to mishandling by the employee.
- Unemployment compensation, severance pay or legal fees.
- Recruitment and training costs which you must incur again to replace the employee.

We remember a business owner who shared his challenge with us. He had hired an employee as a desk clerk in a small hotel. The candidate seemed suitable for the position. Within the first week, he found out that she was being rude to the guests and quite often even got into arguments with them.

Obviously he could not afford to keep her. This was not a training issue. This person was totally unsuitable for a customer service job. He fired her, but guess what? She filed a lawsuit against him! He was then forced to spend his valuable time, money and energy fighting the lawsuit.

If you think that these are rare occurrences, I am sure you are either extremely lucky or have not hired enough people yet.

We also find a number of managers who have never been trained in hiring make mistakes that could easily have been avoided. On the other hand, they can cause extensive damage by hiring the wrong person or being sued.

Many managers have asked candidates questions which could easily have been fodder for discrimination lawsuits.

Hopefully, you know that you cannot ask questions like:

a. Are you married?

b. Are you pregnant?

c. What are your child care arrangements?

d. In what year did you graduate from high school/college?

e. Are you a U.S. citizen?

f. Have you ever been arrested?

during the interview process. Check with the U.S. Equal Employment Opportunity Commission's Web site www.eeoc.gov for clarity on such issues.

The simple idea is *"Hire slowly and Fire quickly."*

Certain states have laws that favor employees.

While traveling on an airplane recently, we talked to a manager who oversees employees in eight states. About 400 employees report to her. She made it her job to understand the intricacies of California law as it relates to hiring and firing. She documents everything so that if she has to fire an employee, she is protected and so is the company.

Our goal is not to scare you about hiring but we do want to make you aware of the minefield that being an employer is.

Case History:
Real Estate Agent's Assistant

To give you another example, a real estate agent who was referred to us was looking to hire a new assistant. He had hired two employees previously but they had not worked out. During our conversation, we found out that this real estate agent had been a staffing director in his previous career.

Because of his background, he was quite surprised that he had made bad hiring decisions. After we probed into his process of hiring, we found that he was not using personality-style assessments and he did not test the skills of the candidates. Why was he missing these components?

The reason was that in his previous employment, he was part of a team that did the testing and interviews. Now he was required to do all of that himself, and being a busy business owner, he simply skipped some of the steps.

This time he used the recommended process and he is extremely confident of the success of his hire. He has done his due diligence and has collected all the necessary information before making the job offer.

This only illustrates that hiring is something most sales professionals and business owners are not ready for. Very few professionals have any idea of when they should hire or who they should hire. In most cases that we have encountered, business owners and managers believe that anybody can help them and can be trained in no time! So let us find out if you are ready to hire . . .

Are You Ready To Hire?

Simply circle Yes or No to each question:

1	Do you know the best and highest value use of your time?	Yes/No
2	Do you have a clear vision of your organization/department?	Yes/No
3	Do you have a clear, visual plan of processes in the organization/department?	Yes/No
4	Are these processes assigned to specific employees?	Yes/No
5	Do you have detailed job description for each position?	Yes/No

6	Do you have a compensation structure that motivates your employees for best performance?	Yes/No
7	Do you have a proven system in place to attract the best employees?	Yes/No
8	Do you have a proven system to identify the best candidate among the applicants?	Yes/No
9	Do you have a 90-day plan to orient and train your new hire?	Yes/No
10	Do you have a performance evaluation system in place for your employees?	Yes/No

If you have answered "No" to any question, then we encourage you to do the homework and prepare for the hiring process. This work cannot be done by other people for you.

You might use a coach or a consultant to help you in any or all of these areas. The sooner you complete this task, the better it is for you and the employees on your team. We have already mentioned how expensive it is to make a bad hire.

Worse than making a bad hire is hiring a quality person but not being able to retain the talent.

Chapter 2
Common Mistakes in Hiring

One of the biggest challenges we find is that sales professionals and business owners think they can find somebody who is both people-oriented and great on follow-through and detailed work.

We all have strengths and weaknesses. To assume you will find somebody who does not have any flaws is plain ignorance.

Here are five common mistakes employers make in hiring:

1. "I need a body right now."

The manager hires out of desperation. This is common when the manager finds himself overwhelmed. Maybe somebody just quit or the manager received a number of leads and does not know how to get the transactions closed or tasks accomplished.

At such a time the prevailing thinking is that anybody can fit the bill or that it is better to have somebody then nobody. Unfortunately we have met managers who have hired people out of desperation and the employee turns out to be a completely wrong fit.

Why? Very simply, when you are in a desperate mode, you are not thinking clearly. You are so focused on filling the position that you end up hiring anybody who promises you the world. You overestimate the credentials of the applicant and your ability and skills as a manager.

Recently a client hired an individual who should have been tested more thoroughly. This candidate sounded good and said everything that the client wanted to hear. We had some reservations during the hiring process but the client had no other candidate. We advised that if he is willing to take the risk, then he should go ahead and hire but monitor the new employee closely.

Unfortunately the client had not done that particular job in such a long time that he was not competent to train and supervise the individual. We did not know that.

Needless to say, this individual created numerous problems and was totally unable to perform the job. He was immediately terminated but he had done quite a bit of irreparable damage by upsetting customers and failing to close the transactions.

2. Hiring close family, friends or referrals without any evaluation.

We have known a client for a while and she comes back with pretty much the same problem each time. She seems to always have employee friction problems in her team. Unfortunately, she has not been coachable enough to listen to what we have to say and implement the ideas.

The biggest problem is that she continues to hire her close friends and family members without evaluating whether they are the best fit for the position. It seems to create conflict between different employees – those who are favored because they are hired based on their relationship to the owner and those who are from outside the close family and friend circle.

She finds it difficult to motivate and get any worthwhile performance out of these employees. Teamwork is a struggle and she seems frustrated. She feels that there is a magic bullet which will solve her problems.

Unless she starts hiring the person who is most suitable for the position instead of using nepotism, she will always have this challenge.

3. No process to screen candidates.

Most sales professionals and managers are quick decision makers and do not have the necessary patience to do the due diligence before hiring people. It sounds simple, but it is hard for people who pride themselves on their quick thinking and decision-making ability to slow down and go through all the steps necessary to get well-qualified people.

Why is this attitude a major business risk? Just using your gut feel to make a hiring decision is not a smart idea. Why? Again, most managers are not trained in this skill.

It is not a coincidence that Kim went through formal training during her bachelor's degree in Human Resource Development. She had to conduct numerous interviews and she was evaluated based on the videotape and transcripts of these interviews.

This process of hiring without enough understanding of screening candidates can be hazardous. Business owners and managers must understand that hiring should not be based on intuition alone.

4. Hiring the candidate who is just like you.

This individual reminds you of yourself when you were younger. You have a good "gut" feeling about this person.

Many managers tend to hire a person with whom they feel comfortable. Of course, you like people who are like you or remind you of yourself. If the candidate is too much like you, then why are you hiring your clone? It is rarely a good idea to hire your clone.

Sales people are great at building rapport. We know that it is easy to feel close to somebody just like you. At that moment the job description takes a back seat and the pleasing personality of the individual becomes the focus. What are the pitfalls of hiring somebody just like you?

As we mention later, there are certain traits which are common to high achievers; one of them is the ability to make quick decisions with very little analysis and follow through. Gut instinct plays a bigger role than carefully collected data.

In such circumstances, the manager is blinded to the fact that he needs a person who complements his style, not someone who is a mirror image. If both people on the team fail to analyze data and have no commitment to follow through, the end result is not difficult to guess.

5. You hate to do the work that you should be doing.

Let us say that you hate detailed paper work and you are poor in following through. You feel that all you need to do is to hire somebody who likes that work and is competent at it and your worries will go away.

Don't make that mistake. Before you hire such a person, learn the basics of that job for two reasons. One reason is that the person who walks in to do that job will definitely need you to give her orientation and training before she can be productive. Secondly, that person's style of work will differ from your style by necessity. If you cannot appreciate her role and how she functions, you will be a poor manager.

We know managers who hire out their weaknesses and, because they have not had the patience to master those skills themselves, they are inept at training and supervising that person. Therefore, they end up losing that person.

We distinctly remember one loan officer who has had a revolving door of hiring and then losing employees. She believes that the new employee can function on her own with little or no supervision and training. Because of her extremely direct and bottom-line communicating style, she has lost a number of good employees who became very frustrated. Unless she understands her role as a manager, she won't be able to keep a quality person.

Here are some of the myths about being a manager and hiring:

- It is easy to find a good employee.
- The market is full of people who are looking to work for you.
- You need very little knowledge about screening candidates.
- Interviewing is a natural skill and you can conclude how the person will perform with just the resume and an interview.
- You must sell the person on how good the job is.
- You don't have to train and the employee can learn quickly on his own.
- All employees are aware of what they do well.
- Employees are self-motivated and need very little incentive to do quality work.
- Employees can hold themselves accountable and need very little supervision.
- All employees understand your communication style and priorities.
- A candidate who shows confidence means the person is competent to do the job and I don't have to check the candidate's competency.

Don't worry. This book will assist you in understanding the profile of the person you need to hire and how to go about identifying the person who has the traits that will help you in putting together a winning team.

Don't believe everything your candidate tells you!

❏ A sales candidate will tell you he/she is "money motivated".
A candidate will always tell you what you want to hear.
You can dangle a million dollar bonus and still not motivate
a "non-money motivated" person.

❏ A sales candidate will tell you he/she has no "fear of
rejection" and loves making calls and prospecting.
Many managers fail to check with the former employers
to validate the candidate's past performance and track
record. We must admit that sometimes past managers are
reluctant to give "poor" recommendations. Yet you must
seek references and verify them the best way you can.

❏ An administrative assistant candidate will tell you he/she
loves paperwork.
You might end up hiring someone who wants to deal
with the people aspect of the job and not the paperwork
part. Paperwork ends up being neglected.

❏ A candidate will tell you he/she is very organized.
Some candidates are naturally organized. It is a skill and
a natural tendency. But it is hard to develop the skill when
you don't have the required aptitude for it. Despite best
intentions, it is difficult to make a duck fly!

❏ A candidate will tell you he/she is coachable.
We remember an incident where a manager was very
keen to hire a sales person candidate. This person seemed
aggressive and had actually brought a couple of leads
during the interview. You would hire that person, wouldn't
you?

We administered an assessment that showed that he was not coachable. So we asked the managers involved to contact the previous employer to find out if the person was coachable or not.

His previous manager's reaction was: "Follow instructions? He made up his own!" Unfortunately, the company still ended up hiring him and within 90 days, he had to be fired. The reason was that he had a second business which consumed more of his time and he was not fully dedicated to his employer.

❐ A candidate will tell you he/she is willing to follow rules and procedures.

❐ A candidate will tell you he/she is a loyal team player and wants stability.

❐ A candidate will tell you he/she has clear and focused goals.

❐ A candidate will tell you he/she he wants to be trained and wants to learn and grow.

Some candidates truly enjoy learning and want to grow. Some candidates are more ambitious and want to learn from you and then leave you for better opportunities. Do you want to end up training your competitors' employees?

We were helping a mortgage broker who had an excellent candidate. This candidate did not have mortgage experience, but had been a star salesperson in his previous jobs. He had his own landscaping business during his college days and was clearly an ambitious person.

After we administered an assessment that revealed his motivators, we found that he was money-motivated and also keen to be his own boss. That is a red flag for us. This could mean that he would learn from our client and would very likely end up setting up his own shop. Our client could understand why that would be the case based on his employment history and he decided to not hire him.

Wouldn't you think that if somebody had been a loan processor for twenty years, they should be pretty good, right? Wrong. One of our clients, Lynn Rogers, a mortgage consultant, had hired a loan processor who had twenty years experience in the field. We had reservations about the candidate's willingness to follow rules and her aptitude to do detailed paperwork.

Lynn was shocked that somebody with such vast experience as a processor would have any issues related to paperwork. She ended up hiring her and had to fire her after she found out that this person was causing more problems than solving them. Needless to say, Lynn now does not hire without making sure that the candidate has a favorable report.

Chapter 3
Why High Achievers Fail As Managers

It is exciting to move into the next stage of your growth as an achiever and that is to be a great manager and leader of people. We have found some interesting paradoxes. (This chapter was a combined project with Stan Mann of A Solution Coaching & Training, LLC, Livonia, MI, www.stanmann.com)

The very traits that have helped high achievers in their success can prevent them from being great managers and even greater leaders.

We would like to share with you these seven traits and what you can do about them.

1. High achievers know their purpose and role in the team and, therefore, do not need anybody's help in setting their goals. However, *most* employees *do* need help in clarifying goals and objectives.

It is important to provide detailed guidelines for your employees so they know what is expected of them. The manager must provide a checklist of daily and weekly tasks, along with outcomes that are critical to the position. Additionally, the manager must review the checklist before the person starts working.

2. High achievers are highly motivated. They do not need supervision, but most employees do. High achievers often fail to provide the supervision and support to help their employees meet the objectives.

As mentioned before, the checklists must be reviewed daily or weekly, depending on the supervision needed for the position. Daily and weekly team meetings help you monitor and correct the employee before it is too late. Every meeting with your new hire is an opportunity to train regarding company policies and performance guidelines.

3. High achievers use intuition to make decisions in ways that are hard to replicate in employees. Actually, most employees need a structure and a system to help them make decisions.

As a former computer programmer, one of the tools Minesh used is called "decision making flowcharts". This tool guides a programmer through the decision making process of an end-user. It is obviously impossible for the programmer to understand every facet of the job of an end-user so reducing the process to a visual tool, clarifies how the programmer must design the software.

The flowchart is a series of actions with questions which determine what should be the next action. Another tool in management is called the decision-tree. The idea is inherently the same. Every job can be reduced to such a chart.

It is impossible to write every single action and the preceding question, yet it is important to provide enough of this type of documentation that the team member feels comfortable in taking the next step.

Another simple example is that of a recipe. The recipe leaves very little to conjecture, yet the results for two cooks can be different. This is to remind you that even with detailed directions, like in a recipe, it is possible to make mistakes and to get a variety of results. Imagine what would happen without the recipe? So always try to teach your thought process of arriving at conclusions and then what should be the next step to your team members.

4. High achievers believe that profit is the end result and people are resources to help achieve that goal. Unfortunately in such an environment, people feel used and the morale suffers. Hence people do not buy into the vision of the company and perform poorly.

When you hire employees, we recommend that you hire people who are naturally money-motivated. We will discuss motivators later in another chapter. The reason behind this recommendation is that employees who are not money-motivated view people who make a lot of money ('a lot of money' is a very subjective term- we understand) as greedy and selfish people. Be aware that some people view profit as a crime and any such person in your team will begrudge your income.

After you have qualified people on your team, then revisit the company mission and objectives often. Help employees understand their role in making the company successful and how the company's success benefits them.

Recently, Minesh sat down with one of our employees to clarify our vision and outline the importance of his role. Minesh saw his eyes light up as he felt totally connected to the vision. Minesh must have mentioned this information in some other form earlier, but this time it hit home. Thus, repeating your mission statement, vision, and plan for how different people and roles fit together is imperative to create the necessary buy-in of the team members.

5. High achievers make decisions quickly and implement the ideas immediately. Most employees do not feel that they have the authority to make decisions and need guidance in helping implement ideas.

In an excellent book **"Fierce Conversations,"** (Berkley Trade, 2004), Susan Scott explains the concept of teaching decision-making to employees. The key part we learned from the book is that managers need to let the employee learn from mistakes, but they need to make sure that it does not affect the root of the organization.

Focus on making sure that these mistakes do not end up causing huge losses. Ask the employee to involve you when the possible damage could be more than a certain amount of revenue or relationships. The employee must know the boundaries well and must contact you as soon as the he realizes that he could be exceeding his authority.

Teaching employees how to balance responsibility while providing adequate authority to solve the problem is critical to your success as a successful delegator. There is a fine line between trying to micro-manage and not being adequately engaged in the progress of an employee.

6. High achievers are quick to criticize and speak their mind. Most people need to be nurtured and encouraged.

This is a tricky area. In our booklet **"The Secret To Rich And Rewarding Relationships At Work And Home,"** we explain the concept of deposits and withdrawals in relationships. Unless the team member is aware of your communication style, he might not appreciate your comments. People who are direct in their communication style might not realize that the team member might feel intimidated and offended by not only your words but your style of delivery as well.

Despite a tremendous emphasis on self-esteem in our culture, most people might not have enough self-esteem to withstand constructive criticism from the supervisor. Dale Carnegie talks about the "sandwich" method. For every critical comment, he recommends using praise before and after the comment. As a manager, one must realize whether the team member is able to listen without taking the criticism too personally.

We all take comments personally despite our desire to not do so and our understanding that it is only for our good. Being aware of this principle should not prevent the manager from giving his frank input. The point of caution is to make sure that the comment is heard in the proper spirit.

A common problem is that the manager only comments when something goes wrong. Ken Blanchard of **"One Minute Manager"** (HarperCollins Business, 2000) fame calls it the "Zap" method of management. Instead, he suggests catching people when they are doing good work so that they are used to the "One Minute Praise" which makes it easy to give them a "One Minute Reprimand". His other book **"Whale Done"** with Thad Lacinak, Chuck Tompkins, and Jim Ballard (Simon & Schuster, 2002) emphasizes the importance of reinforcing good behavior.

7. High achievers have high self-esteem and hence take failures in their stride. Most people do not have a high enough self-esteem and need to be given avenues to succeed in a stepwise manner.

We have also highlighted this part in trait number six . The key in this challenge is that most people need to have short enough milestones for the big goals. Their self-esteem allows them to see only so far. If you expect them to see the big picture and feel emotionally connected to it automatically just like you, then you are mistaken and will be disappointed and might even be angry toward the employee. They need steps that point them in the direction of the goal.

What might seem like a trivial goal to you might be a big challenge for your team member. So use your judgment to determine whether the team member can focus on the goal that is being set and can feel a sense of urgency in achieving the goal.

Again, having daily and weekly checklists will assist you in providing focus and clarity to the bigger goal in front of the team.

The main point we want you to get from this chapter is that there is a significant difference between high achievers and the majority of employees. This is not meant to denigrate people but to understand the mindset of high achievers – which is a good moniker for most successful business owners and managers. Even more important, it is meant to help high achievers understand the mindset of their employees. If high achievers fail to grasp the difference, then they will fail as managers.

It is a good thing to expect people to succeed, but it is important to figure out where people are and then guide them appropriately.

Chapter 4

Twelve
Simple Hiring
Steps

Here is a simple checklist of hiring steps that are useful in the hiring process. This list is by no means exhaustive, but enables you to have a starting point.

1. Create an extremely detailed job description which also gives a clear idea of what the person must do and how you can hold him accountable. This lets you know quickly whether the person is meeting the expectations set up for that position. The candidate knows his responsibility in advance and there is no confusion even before the person takes on the employment.

2. Let people in your sphere of influence know that you are looking to fill a position and advertise in appropriate places like Craig's List, newspapers etc.

Some areas in the country get great results from online resources like www.Craigslist.com and some don't. You might even use a recruiter but be aware that recruiters might not screen the candidate enough. They get paid for the hire and not for the person working out in the long run. We have heard enough stories where the recruiter brought questionable candidates and, because the manager was busy or trusted the recruiter more than he should have, ended up with employees that did not work out.

After the first 30-60 days, the recruiter fee is paid and you might be stuck with an unwanted employee. So most of my clients, even if they use the recruiter, they still assess the candidates as if the person came off the street.

3. Review all resumes, focusing on candidates with the right background and longevity in a similar capacity. We always recommend candidates who have stayed at a job long enough, that is very similar, to be considered loyal and have mastered the job. In our opinion this period is 2 years or more.

4. Pick three to five candidates and schedule interviews. In some cases, we also recommend conducting preliminary phone-based interviews to see how they sound on the phone. If you feel they are worthwhile candidates, then agree to meet the candidates in person.

5. Check each candidate's credit score. Todd Scrima, President of Summit Funding and a principal coach of The CORE Coaching and Training (www.TheCORE.tv) insists on credit score. He has repeatedly found that people who lack credibility and accountability score low on the credit score. His recommendation is not to hire anybody whose credit score is below 640. He cancels any interview if the candidate's credit score is below 640.

Please note that some lawmakers are trying to end using credit scores in the employment screening process. So find out what is the legal process in using such tools in your state.

6. Interview candidates with a prepared set of questions and take notes during the interview. Instead of trying to sell them on the job, ask questions to determine why they should be considered for the job.

7. Measure the candidates' skill level for the position you are hiring. Talking about possessing a skill is easier than demonstrating it.

We remember one of our clients who was upset when he found out that the new employee was not adequately skilled for the job. Checking their phone skills, having them look over agreements, and asking specific questions about how they will handle a specific problem in their job will give you awareness whether the candidates have the requisite skill.

If the employee will need to use certain software that is specific to his role, have him show you on the computer how he will input data, check conditions, and complete the task.

8. Pick your best two candidates.

9. Use assessments to screen and qualify the candidates. Our recommendations are based on the job description and the information we have collected on the organization so far. We discuss assessments in later chapters.

We highly recommend that managers take assessments as well so the person can fit the manager's style.

10. Schedule an appointment with the expert to review the assessments in detail to analyze the information in these two reports, explain it to you in plain English and let you know whether or not the candidate is the right person 'on the bus' – for your team - and whether or not they will be 'in the right seat' – that is, in the right position for them to succeed.

11. Check references diligently.

12. Don't be in a hurry to make a decision. Evaluate your options carefully. It is okay to restart the process if no candidate fits the requirement. Desperation can cause you to make unfortunate mistakes.

Great companies attract and keep great people. Base your decision on a person's talent and past performance, not on their promises.

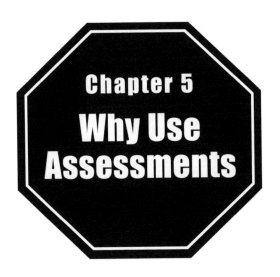

Chapter 5
Why Use Assessments

Case Study :
Real Estate Administrative Assistant

This incident is that of a real estate agent who is a top earning real estate agent in Florida. She has one Buyer's Agent on the team and another support staff person.

She was looking to replace an administrative person who was not organized enough.

The agent ordered assessments for one candidate who had been referred by a friend. The candidate was a licensed real estate agent who did not want to be independent but be part of a team and do more paperwork. The agent loved the candidate. The agent was also desperate to hire an assistant.

The battery of assessments revealed that the candidate had a typical sales person's profile. They showed that the candidate's strengths revealed she was quick, decisive and outgoing. However, her report revealed she would have challenges in the areas of follow through, being organized and attention to paperwork/details.

Our recommendation was to NOT hire the candidate for the position of administrative assistant. The agent was disappointed to hear the outcome based on the assessments used to screen the candidate, as she was really eager to hire the candidate based on her pleasant demeanor and outstanding resume. She was reluctant to hear our recommendation and was determined to hire anyway. We recommended the agent to do two things to verify our findings to support the power of the assessment findings if she was going to hire despite our diagnosis.

One - To verify our findings with the former employer and see if the candidate had good follow through, was organized and filled out paperwork with accuracy and efficiency.

Two - To give the candidate a skill-based test to verify her work skills.

We suggested the agent give the candidate a purchase agreement filled with mistakes. The candidate was asked to make the corrections and make sure all the signatures and initials are made in the correct places on the purchase agreement.

A month later, the agent called to order another assessment. We asked, why? She had hired the candidate against our recommendation. She said she was desperate and really felt that it would work out. The new employee had made errors on a purchase agreement and clearly did not know how to fill out a purchase agreement correctly despite having been an agent for at least a year.

Whatever we had predicted about the candidate's abilities came true. Since then, this real estate agent has used our services without hesitation and reluctance. She understands the power of the assessments and listens carefully to the information we share.

Assessments are Used By All Major Companies

Most employees expect to be tested before being hired. The more established the company, the more likely the expectation of assessments. For a major company, an employee is likely to go through a series of tests and assessments over a period of two or more days before being offered the job.

The frequent question in the minds of some managers is what can an assessment tool give me that I can't get by screening resumes and interviewing candidates with good background and references? This is a very important question and it is likely that you have this question as well. Let us mention just a couple of challenges in screening candidates without using assessment tools.

The first is Minesh's own experience. Minesh was a bright student in engineering and has a bachelor's and a master's degree from prestigious institutions in India. He did well in school and chose computer programming as his profession.

Though he liked certain challenges in his profession, he seldom felt fulfilled. His strength was in communication and people interaction. Sitting in a cubicle or a separate office, programming all day long was emotionally draining.

After twelve years of a career in software consulting, he knew it was time to start a career that he really enjoyed. His passions include speaking, writing, and coaching. The transition was not easy, to say the least.

The first time he took the behavioral profile (administered by his friend Stan Mann) he was amazed at how accurate the results were. The report clearly showed him to be a people-oriented person with much less inclination towards detailed paper work and follow through. He likes to moves from project to project and loves new challenges. He has never met a stranger and finds himself comfortable talking to anybody he meets.

Today if he was to wear a manager's hat and see if he is fit for the "programmer" role, he would not hire himself. Today he is fulfilled and loves the freedom from the routines of his previous career.

The key reason we are mentioning Minesh's experience is that had he taken these assessments when he was embarking on his engineering career, he would have known that he would never feel satisfied and would always feel uncomfortable in the highly structured, detail-oriented culture of an engineering profession.

His excellent academic credentials and ability to be articulate in interviews had convinced all his employers to hire him, but he knew within himself that this was not the profession for him.

In the last interview that he had in engineering, the committee of five managers was convinced that he was extremely sharp, knowledgeable, and articulate. They were ready to offer him the job but he called to let them know that he was not interested in the position - and he never went to another interview in the programming field.

We hope this helps you understand that it is possible that you could be doing a favor to your potential employees by not hiring them for the position that they are really not suited for.

Overcoming Your Skepticism of Assessments

Even some human resource professionals are not familiar with assessments. Some are just skeptical of the value they bring during the hiring process.

The most convincing element we have seen is when we offer for the manager to take an assessment. After the manager reads his own report, he is usually quite impressed and realizes that he has an excellent tool to understand the candidate and also his present employees.

If you have never taken an assessment like the ones we shall be covering in subsequent chapters, we recommend that you take one yourself. Take time to go over the report and see how you can use it in hiring and managing employees. These assessments will also help you in finding out how to best communicate with others and they can also learn how to communicate with you.

One of the companies whose products we use to assist our clients is Target Training International (TTI) located in Scottsdale, AZ. These are some of the results which organizations around the world have obtained by using their assessment tools.

- One company ran 800 people through the Success Discovery Process and had a 50% increase in employee satisfaction.
- Another company ran reports but did not go over the reports on a one-to-one basis and still showed a 26% increase in employee satisfaction.
- Another company was losing 50% of their new hires during the training program. Benchmarking the job and bringing in the right people increased the retention to 80%.
- An organization had a 74% turnover in their sales force. After benchmarking and debriefing, they reduced that number to zero during the last 18 months.
- A mortgage company was experiencing over 300% turnover annually among their sales department. The position was benchmarked and the top five sales people were compared to the benchmark. Turnover was reduced 250% in just 6 months after they used the TriMetrix® System for their hiring standard.
- A service organization was losing 60% of all new hires during their first 60 days on the job. Using TTI tools, they changed the hiring process resulting in no turnover for the last 60 days.

One of the most important reasons for using such assessments is that they bring objectivity to your hiring process. It is possible for you to meet a candidate and due to certain similarities between you and the candidate, you are biased towards the candidate. Maybe you attended the same school, go to the same church or have common interests like skiing. After the person takes the assessment, you have brought additional information that does not have such personal prejudice or bias.

When an outside professional examines the reports, she has no such bias. Her focus is to provide you with all the necessary information to help you decide whether this candidate is likely to get the job done or not.

Isn't that what you want? Do you want to hire a person you like just based on common interests or somebody who stays with you for a long time and becomes a valuable asset to your team?

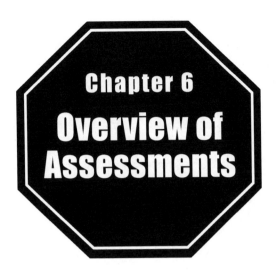

Common "Personality" Assessment Models

What makes us different? One way of classifying people that appears in many systems of "personality" profiling is to determine a person's preferences in terms of how they perceive and respond to the world.

Below are some of the more popular models.

- The 16 Personality Factors is described by Raymond Cattell in the 1930's.
- Sigmund Freud's Theory of Personality Factors includes the concepts of Id, Ego, and Cathexis which set the stage for the classic understanding of personality.
- The Minnesota Multiphasic Personality Inventory (MMPI) is one of the most frequently used tools to assess clinical psychiatric conditions in the mental health fields.
- Type A and Type B Personalities. Are you prone to heart attacks or not? A simple division of preference or personality type is into Type A and Type B, which is based broadly on anxiety and stress levels.

- Kolbe's Learning Style describes four learning styles: divergers, convergers, accommodators and assimilators based on two preference dimensions: perception and processing.
- David Keirsey's Temperament Sorter assessment tool is based on the Carl Gustav Jung Type Inventory Model. His work is described in his book "Please Understand Me II".
- MBTI® or The Myers-Briggs Type Inventory was created by the mother-daughter team of Katherine Briggs and Isobel Briggs Myers. It's a modern system to identify a person's type based on the Carol Gustav Jung Type Inventory Model. It is probably the most popular typing system in the world today next to the DISC.
- DISC Model was created by William Moulton Marston in 1928 to describe human behaviors based on a four dimensions: Dominance, Inducement, Steadiness, and Compliance.

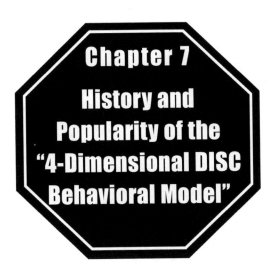

Chapter 7

History and Popularity of the "4-Dimensional DISC Behavioral Model"

(The history is based on an article written by Russell J. Watson, Ed.D. of Target Consultants, Inc.)

Some type of four-dimensional model of behavior has been in existence since the beginning of time starting with Empodocles (air, earth, fire, and water), Hippocrates (sanguine, choleric, phlegmatic, and melancholic), followed by the modern thinking of Carl Jung in 1921 (thinking, feeling, sensing, and intuiting), and Dr. William Moulton Marston in 1928 (Dominance, Inducement, Steadiness, and Compliance). Currently there are more than a dozen DISC-type models in the marketplace, and since the DISC concept is in the public domain, other variations might continue to emerge.

The DISC model has been of enormous benefit in determining the **_how_** of our behavioral choices or style preferences. These uses include coaching, placement, management, team-building, enhancing work performance, enriching family relationships and numerous other practical uses. The DISC model is not a "personality test." The DISC model describes four basic traits within our personality but the term "personality" describes a larger and more complex set of characteristics that distinguishes an individual that goes beyond four behavioral traits. As a result, you will see variations of this four dimensional model called: Type, Style, Preferences, and many other terms related to components of personality. However, most of the models avoid the use of the word "personality".

The DISC model is one of the most widely used non-clinical behavioral instruments in the marketplace, and it has gained wide acceptance in the US, Europe, Australia, New Zealand, and South Africa. Its success comes in large part from its ease of use and interpretation and the memorable and pronounceable name, DISC.

What all of the DISC models have in common is that they attempt to describe observable behavior, that is, _how_ someone does what he does. If you are a salesperson, _how_ do you sell? Do you sell as a high or low D, I, S, or C, or most likely, a combination thereof? If you are a manager, _how_ do you manage? As a D, I, S, or C, or a combination?

In the workplace, we use the DISC model to measure how a person will behave and perform in the workplace.

General Characteristics of "Dominant, Influential, Steady and Cautious Model" (DISC)

DISC is a behavioral model that measures and describes "HOW" a person acts in life, or the manner of how a person does things in life. There are 4 dimensions or styles measured: Dominant, Influential, Steady and Cautious. People with similar styles tend to exhibit specific types of behavior common to that style. Much of a person's behavior comes from "nature" (inherent), and the rest comes from "nurture" (our upbringing). The DISC model merely analyzes behavioral style; that is, a person's manner of doing things.

We can use an assessment tool to measure and describe a person's behavioral style to determine the intensity level of each of the four dimensions Dominant, Influential, Steady and Cautious. . We can measure each dimension, and give it a value anywhere between zero and 100. A zero value means the person has the least characteristics attributed to the behavioral style and 100 means the person has the most characteristics attributed to the behavioral style. Within each dimension, we can define each dimension with descriptive, observable behavioral characteristics or traits. These traits are measured in words to express intensity in each type. These words are objective and descriptive rather than subjective and judgmental. This means that DISC shows a pattern in how we act.

Dominant (D):

What it measures: Dominant measures how a person responds to problems and challenges.

What *High D* Dominant implies: A **high Dominant** person (D) has a score higher than 50, is an extrovert, task-oriented person who is, **direct, driven, demanding, determined, decisive,** and a **doer**.

What *Low D* Dominant implies: A **low Dominant** person (D) has a score less than 50, is a person who takes more time to analyze a situation before making a decision and has a more low-keyed, pleasant, agreeable behavior style.

Strengths of a Person Having a Dominant Behavioral Style: Active, Outgoing, Independent, Persistent, Direct, Energetic, Busy and Fearless.

Best Management Technique: Ask "What" kind of questions.

Weaknesses of a Person Having a Dominant Behavioral Style: Tends to focus on own goals rather than people; tends to "tell" rather than "ask" and can be too demanding.

Influential (I):

What it measures: Influential measures how a person influences others to bring them to his own point of view.

What *High I* Influential implies: A high Influential person (I) has a score 50 or higher, is an extroverted, people-oriented person who is **inducing, inspiring, impressive, interacting** and **interesting**.

What does *Low I* Influential implies: A **low Influential** person (I) has a score less than 50, is a more reflective, factually based person who likes to persuade others by logic. Low influencing people tend to be more guarded and undemonstrative about sharing their feelings or giving trust to others who they don't know well.

Strengths of a Person Having an Influential Behavioral Style: Can build rapport quickly; and is highly social, persuasive, friendly, energetic, busy, optimistic, imaginative; and tends to focus on the new and the future.

Best Management Technique: Ask "Who?" kind of questions.

Weaknesses of a Person Having an Influential Behavioral Style: Can be overly confident; is distractible; does not pay attention to some details; tends to be a poor time manager; and focuses on people rather than tasks.

Steady (S):

What it measures: Steady measures how a person responds to the pace of the environment.

What *High S* Steady implies: A **high Steady** person (S) has a score 50 or higher, is an introverted, people-oriented person who is **submissive, stable, supportive, shy, enjoys status-quo** and **enjoys being a specialist**.

What *Low S* implies: A **low Steady** person (S) with a score less than 50, is someone who likes to work in a fast-paced environment with a variety of tasks that can change often and he can adapt quickly to new changes.

Strengths of a Person Having a Steady Behavioral Style: Enjoys consistency and stability; is accommodating and peace-seeking; likes helping and supporting others; tends to be a good listener and counselor; and enjoys close relationships with a few friends.

Weaknesses of a Person Having a Steady Behavioral Style: Unable to set priorities, can be non-emotional at times, can be a little too slow in pace at times (does not like to be rushed), and dislikes conflicts.

Best Management Technique:

Ask in a supportive manner, rather than tell; ask "How?" kind of questions

Cautious (C):

What it measures: Cautious measures how a person responds to rules and procedures set by others.

What *High C* Cautious implies: A **high Cautious** person (C) has a score 50 or higher, is an introverted, task-oriented person who is **conscientious, compliant, correct, calculating, concerned, careful** and **contemplative**.

What *Low C* Cautious implies: A **low Cautious** person (C) with a score less than 50, is someone who tends to be careless with details that are not important to him. This person might see rules set by other people as not "rules" but guidelines and be very independent about observing "rules" and not be too concerned about the facts.

Strengths of a Person Having a Cautious Behavioral Style: Tends to be a slow & critical thinker, perfectionist, logical, fact-based, highly organized, and a follower of rules.

Best Management Technique: Ask '"Why?" kinds of questions.

Weaknesses of a Person Having a Cautious Behavioral Style: Can be overly critical and obsessive about getting things done the "correct way"; often gets overwhelmed by details which causes this person to lose priority and be too slow; tend to be very private and not show feelings to others; and can tend to view situations with fear.

Key Notes about DISC Report:

1. It only tells you a person's communication and behavior style. It does not tell you whether the person will sell. The DISC does not measure a person's intelligence, technical skills, or selling skills.
2. It does not predict if an outgoing person will prospect.
3. If you have too many high Dominants (D's) on your team, it can be disastrous as they are all impatient and not very communicative.
4. Having a person with Steadiness (S) behavior type is critical as they have a tempering effect and typically do not like change. They also tend to be more loyal.
5. A good team will have a balanced set of styles instead of having all of the same style.
6. Having a particular behavior styles is not considered "bad" or "good". Each person brings his own unique set of strengths and weakness based on the behavior style plus own talent, skills, life experiences and maturity.

How should you use the report?

1. If you could pick one characteristic – which one would you chose?

    a. People-oriented or Task/result-oriented

    b. Fast paced or Slow paced?

2. Do not expect people to have a great outgoing personality and simultaneously to be great at paper work or follow through.

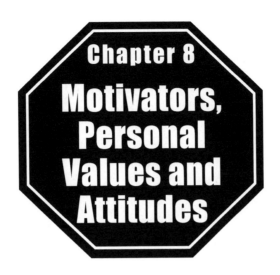

Chapter 8

Motivators, Personal Values and Attitudes

Defining Attitudes

In 1928, Eduard Spranger wrote a book entitled **"Types of Men."** He identified six major attitudes or world-views. These attitudes are a type of window through which we view the world and seek fulfillment in our lives. If we are participating in a discussion, activity, or career that is in alignment with our attitudes, we will value or appreciate the experience. On the other hand, if we are in a conversation, activity or career that is in conflict with our dominant attitudes, we will be indifferent or even negative towards the experience, possibly causing stress.

Spranger's model measures 6 major values or attitudes that motivate or drive human beings. Our values inspire or drive us into action. Motivators or values are often called "hidden motivators" as they are not readily observable. Based on Spranger's work, today we can use an assessment tool to uncover a person's motivators and see how it best fits within the work environment.

Motivation Concepts Based on Spranger's 6 Major Values and Attitudes:

1. LEARNING: *The desire to learn and to discover knowledge and truth.* A person enjoys learning for the sake of learning and to master areas of interest. Taken to the extreme, a person might be focused on learning theory at the expense of practicality.

2. MONEY: *The desire to be practical and see tangible results.* A person has the desire for efficiency, utility; to see return on investment or receive personal gain in the form of money, time, energy or resources. Taken to the extreme, the desire to see financial gain can be at the expense of personal relationships.

3. BEAUTY or HARMONY: *The need to appreciate the beauty, nature, form, and the harmony of the surrounding environment.* A person desires personal growth and development and seeks a balanced life. Taken to the extreme, the desire to experience and enjoy all the sense, feelings and impressions can be overwhelming and be stressful for the person.

4. ALTRUISM: *The desire to create strong personal and harmonious relationships with others.* This person has a desire to help people in need and seeks opportunities to serve others. Taken to the extreme, giving the benefit to others may come at a great personal sacrifice or expense.

5. POWER OR POLITICAL: *The desire to obtain personal power and leadership to control own destiny and/or the destiny of others.* This is a person who enjoys influencing or persuading people and could be seen as a great leader. Taken to the extreme, a person's advancement could be at the expense of others and the person could be viewed as a tyrant.

6. RELIGIOUS/SYSTEM FOR LIVING/PRINCIPLE: *The desire to search for a higher purpose in life while living and*

standing firm with own code of conduct. Often this person has a desire to live out a mission or a worthy cause. Taken to the extreme, a person with a firm system of beliefs might not be open to a new set of beliefs.

The "Why" Behind Your Behavior and Actions

What is it that motivates you to take action? What is the source of your desire to become involved in certain activities—or to avoid them? Why do you behave in the manner you do?

The answers lie deep within your unique set of personal interests, attitudes, and values. These powerful motivating forces within you largely affect how you behave and how others perceive you. Identifying them is important to understanding what makes you effective, satisfied, and personally successful.

Key Notes about Using Motivators in Hiring:

- All of your employees might have "Money" as one of the top two motivators (if motivators are close enough, then it could be one of the top three motivators).

Why? In a business environment where profit determines the success of the business, money-motivated individuals are focused on making money for themselves and the company. They are constantly evaluating whether a task or a relationship is worth their investment of time, money and energy.

- For a customer service position, having "Altruism" is a plus.
- If you need a person to learn different aspects of the business in detail, "Learning" would be an added benefit.

We have worked with quite a few people in the financial advising and insurance business. These businesses have ongoing requirements to master changes within the industry.

The "Series 7" license is a challenging one and requires quite a bit of effort on the advisor's part. If the advisor is not motivated to learn, then the advisor will find the examinations to be stressful and might fail repeatedly. If you feel that the new team member will have to learn quite a few new processes and products, this motivator can be critical to their success.

- Motivators of your team members must be closely aligned to your motivators. Being dramatically opposed could cause challenges.

For example if you are a high "Money" motivated individual and the employee is not, then the employee is not likely to understand why you are money-motivated and the employee might think that you are "greedy and selfish." As mentioned before, people who have extremely low "money-motivation" might view profit as a dirty word. In their world, "profit" can take on the meaning that "the person likes to take advantage of other people."

- If an employee has a low "religious/system for living/ principle" and you as the manager have a high "religious/ system for living/principle", then the employee might perceive you as "dogmatic and inflexible".
- If you, as the manager, have low "Beauty or Harmony" and your employees have a high "Beauty and Harmony", they will think of you, as being "too frugal, not focused on having a pleasant and harmonious working environment."

"Valuing" Your Life and the Lives of Others

After you are aware of the dominant attitudes contributing passion and purpose to your life, you will be able to clarify what drives your actions, and what causes conflict.

For example, if you are currently questioning whether you are in the right career, knowing your attitudes will help you decide whether such is the case or not.

We met an owner of a bowling alley making a comfortable living from his business, yet he felt an unease and discontent with his profession. After a deep discussion about his personal values and belief system, we came to find out he was a man who believes in the concepts of having a close personal relationship with God, having a strong and close family relationship, and he thought smoking, swearing and drinking were destructive habits. The reason why his clients like to go to his bowling alley was so they could smoke, swear, and drink beer and get a break from the family. He felt a deep conflict in his life where his business was promoting things he personally did not value. He ended up selling his business and moving into a new career that aligned with his belief systems and motivators.

In addition, applying an understanding of attitudes to your relationships with others will deepen your appreciation of them and clarify the "why" of your interactions.

Results and Benefits

The knowledge you gain from using a motivator assessment tool will help you take control of your decisions, your life's direction and your appreciation of others.

You will:

- Know the WHY of your automatic reactions
- Make career choices that are more in line with your underlying passions
- Understand the causes of conflict in your life
- Develop an increased appreciation for each of the six attitudes
- Gain the flexibility of being able to see life from different viewpoints
- Increase your satisfaction and fulfillment in life

Examples of How To Use Motivators To Reward Employees in the Workplace:

- **LEARNING–Motivated Employee:** When a production goal is reached, the employee can be given an opportunity to take advanced training in a job related field such as attending a one-day computer class for an administrative assistant, or attending a one-day sales skill seminar for sales person, or attending a personal development program or a work-related conference. You might also give a seasoned employee an opportunity to train (teach) new employees.
- **MONEY–Motivated Employee:** When a production goal is reached, the employee can be rewarded based on performance outcomes:
    1) Monetary bonus and/or commission
    2) A gift card or gift certificate to favorite retail store or service
    3) A weekend trip to nearby vacation destination
    4) A special employee appreciation party/dinner/picnic
    5) Time off or end the work day early

- **BEAUTY OR HARMONY–Motivated Employee:** When production goal is reached, the employee can be given an opportunity to create, to decorate or be in charge of a client event.

Examples:
1) Be in charge of organizing the corporate-sponsored day at the ball park, kid's day or family movie night
2) Be in charge of decorating the seminar or conference room for client seminars
3) Be in charge of a customer appreciation party/dinner/picnic
4) Be allowed to "jazz up" the corporate marketing flyer or newsletter

- **ALTRUISM–Motivated Employee:** When production goal is reached the employee can:
    1) Work on a charity event on behalf of the employer
    2) Represent the employer at organization such as Habitat for Humanity, Rotary, Kiwanis, Boys and Girls Club etc.
    3) Select the next charity organization for the employer to sponsor

A seasoned employee might be motivated by
    1) An opportunity to welcome and teach new employees coming into the company
    2) An opportunity to assist in creating functions for company employees like luncheons, parties for birthdays, anniversaries, retirements, etc.
    3) An opportunity to select the next event or charity for the employer to sponsor

- **POWER OR POLITICAL–Motivated Employee:** When production goal is reached, an employee can be motivated by the opportunity to attend personal and leadership seminars to work on management skills and develop "soft skills."

Some employees will be looking for a "title" or some advancement in their career such as being promoted to a managerial position. Such individuals like to control their own destiny and also control destiny of others.

- **RELGIOUS/SYSTEM FOR LIVING/PRINCIPLE– Motivated Employee:** An employee with a "principle" motivation needs a venue to express his/her beliefs - if not in the workplace, it must be expressed in his/her personal life.

If the employee's position allows it, let the employee represent the company as the official company spokesperson at a networking group, social group, or a service organization.

If there are no opportunities for an employee to have his/her "principle" motivation met at work, then his/her fulfillment can be met by joining an organization such as a church, a social club, or a service organization after work.

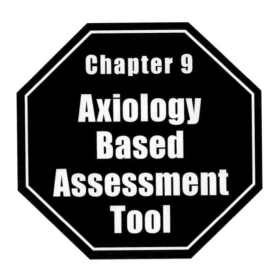

Chapter 9

Axiology Based Assessment Tool

The Need for Talent

Today, business success is measured in TALENT— the RIGHT talent for the job! The lack of job performance and the resultant employee turnover cause missed business opportunities and increased costs. It makes business sense that managers are seeking better ways to accurately assess, develop, and retain top talent.

Using an axiology based assessment tool, an employer can assess an individual's cognitive structure or process of thinking.

What is Axiology? It is a formal system of identifying and measuring value. Axiology is a mathematically based science that objectively identifies how one's mind analyzes and interprets our experiences. It identifies how we are most likely to react in any given situation. It also helps us understand the patterns we use to make judgments. These patterns allow us to translate the results into quantitative measurements and scores, which can in turn be applied to the daily business world.

The pioneer in the field of Axiology is Dr. Robert S. Hartman, who published **"The Structure of Value: Foundation of Scientific Axiology,"** (Southern Illinois, 1967). His work was nominated for the Nobel Peace Prize in 1973. He created an axiology based assessment tool called "The Hartman Value Profile."

The Hartman Value Profile is one of the means by which we are able to measure an individual person's propensity and capacity to value. It is the person's structure of value (the road map and filtration system a person uses to think, evaluate, and make decisions) that results in personality, individual perceptions, and decisions. ***In other words, a person's structure of value is how that person thinks.***

From Dr. Hartman's original work, several assessment companies have created trademark assessment tools to translate scores into capacities related to the business environment.

Using an axiology based assessment tool, an employer can assess an individual's cognitive structure, focusing on three dimensions of thought used in the process of thinking. In the business world, an axiology based assessment tool can answer questions no other tool answers.

The questions answered by using an axiology based assessment tool:

1. How likely will the person be able to take ideas and move them into implementation?
2. How fast will the person be a top performer?
3. How does a person think? Does the person think in real, concrete terms at this moment in time?
4. Will the person be able to perform on the job?
5. How does a person feel, understand, and relate to people?
6. How does a person relate to rules, procedures and structure? Does the person like to follow structure?
7. Does the person understand there are rules in life or not? Or is the person a maverick who likes to make up his own rules?
8. Is the person's concept or perception about his self clear and focused?

9. Does the person have confidence in where he/she is going in life?

10. Does the person have clarity and focus in life at this moment in time? Or is the person searching for a purpose in life?

An axiology based assessment tool can determine a person's capacity on "soft skills" such as empathy, leadership, making decisions, confidence, etc. that is very critical to job performance. If the "soft skill" talent has been developed by the person and is necessary for the job, the person will be very effective. If job performance is lower than desired for a current employee, it could be that the talent or soft skills has not been developed fully, and you, the employer, have an opportunity to develop and ultimately retain top talent by providing job training on specific "soft skills" critical to superior job performance.

Listed below are examples of significant "soft skills" that can be measured by an axiology based assessment tool.

Accountability	Adaptability	Analysis of Information
Attention to Detail	Conflict	Communication
Decisiveness	Delegation	Development of Subordinates
Entrepreneurial	Flexibility	Independence
Initiative	Innovation	Insight
Leadership/Influence	Learning/Self-Improvement	Listening
Making Sound Judgment	Motivation	Organizational Sensitivity
Planning and Organizing	Practical Learning	Presentation Skills
Rapport Building	Resilience	Risk Taking
Sales Persuasiveness	Sensitivity to Others	Strategic Analysis
Stress	Teamwork	Work Standards

Application

Using an axiology based assessment tool can assist executives, managers and employers responsible for others in numerous business processes that require effective talent management, including:

+ *Employee Selection*

    For discovering the strengths and weaknesses of potential employees

+ *Employee Development*

    For discovering the strengths and weaknesses of their associates

    For identifying areas where additional training might be needed

+ *Employee Retention*

    For retaining existing employees and hiring people who are likely to stay in their jobs, thus cutting down significantly on replacement and training costs

+ *Coaching and Mentoring*
+ *Leadership Development*

    For building work teams and groups

    For determining suitability for promotions and job reallocations

Weaving the Assessment Tools Together

The **DISC** assessment tool measures *HOW* a person ACTS.

The **Motivators** assessment tool measures *WHY* a person DOES something.

The **Axiology** assessment tool measures *HOW* a person THINKS.

Taken together we gain a better picture of the employee using the three assessments than we ever could if they were used alone.

People love to use the DISC assessment tool but often forget to use the Motivators and Axiology assessment tools as well.

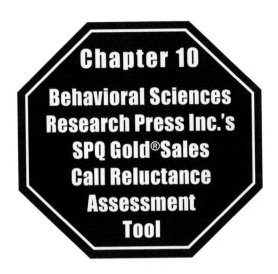

Chapter 10

Behavioral Sciences Research Press Inc.'s SPQ Gold®Sales Call Reluctance Assessment Tool

(Source: "The Psychology Of Sales Call Reluctance®"
by Dudley and Goodson)

Recommended for Sales Positions

What Is Sales Call Reluctance®?

Sales call reluctance® refers to the hesitation or inability to initiate contact with prospective buyers in sufficient numbers. Sales call reluctance® is far more than the fear of making cold calls or using the telephone, sales call reluctance® obstructs all forms of prospecting for new business. And it is expensive.

Each year, sales call reluctance® single-handedly accounts for over half of all failures in one of the largest professions in the world. Across industries, eighty percent of all beginning salespeople fail to complete one year in sales despite the product they sell, the sales training they receive, or their personal belief in the value of the product or service they represent. Sales call reluctance® also influences the productivity of veteran salespeople.

Why Use SPQ Gold® Sales Call Reluctance Assessment?

For new hire:

It is highly recommended that any potential sales candidate to take the **"SPQ Gold® Sales Call Reluctance"** assessment by Behavioral Sciences Research Press Inc. (BSRP) of Dallas, TX, to see if the candidate has any hesitation such as making calls, making contacts, following up with prospects, yielding to prospects/clients, or asking for referrals etc prior to being hired. There are a total of twelve forms of call reluctance measured on the assessment.

For seasoned sales professionals:

Are you earning what you are worth? If the answer is no, sales call reluctance® could be responsible.

How can you determine you have call reluctance®?

SPQ GOLD® Sales Call Reluctance is the world's only diagnostic instrument specifically designed to detect all twelve forms of call reluctance. **Sales call reluctance® is a career-limiting fear that emotionally limits the number of first contacts people can comfortably make with prospective buyers.**

A salesperson experiencing conflict or hesitation associated with making contact with prospective clients is responsible for more failures in sales than any other single factor. Why? It's simple.

If you don't have enough people to present to, it makes little difference what you have to present or how well you have been trained to present it. Without a steady flow of prospects, raw talent, the "right" personality, ability, expensive brochures, product knowledge, drive, the newest laptops, polished presentation skills, or more momentary considerations like "having a great burning desire to achieve" or "having goal congruence" makes little difference.

Even a "highly motivated" salesperson with sales call reluctance® might not be able to overcome emotional reluctances to make the first contact with a prospective client without first making the diagnosis and then getting assistance from a coach to overcome the reluctance. This emotional hesitation can hold a person hostage to sales inactivity and limit what the sales person could earn.

Bottom line: **"The most reliable predictor of success in sales is the number of contacts initiated with prospective buyers on a consistent basis."** *George W. Dudley and Shannon L. Goodson, authors of "The Psychology of Sales Call Reluctance®:Earning What You're Worth in Sales",* (Behavioral Sciences Research Press, June 1999)

How?

The purpose of the **SPQ GOLD® Sales Call Reluctance** assessment is to measure how likely the person will prospect. The more hesitation or emotional fear a sales person has about making the first move to meet a new contact, the less likely the sales person will be able to convert the prospect into a sales transaction.

Here are some possible areas of hesitation or call reluctance® in prospecting that the **SPQ GOLD® Sales Call Reluctance** report reveals:

- Does the salesperson have a positive view towards contacting prospects?
- Does the salesperson feel prepared enough?

- Does the salesperson keep the sales process simple without being overly concerned about impressing prospects/customers?
- Is the salesperson willing to make group presentations?
- Does the salesperson enjoy selling?
- Is the salesperson persistent and persuasive in asking for commitment from prospects/customers? Will the salesperson close?
- Will the salesperson approach successful people or people in the higher-end target market?
- Will the salesperson approach friends for sales or as a source of referrals?
- Will the salesperson approach family for sales or as a source of referrals?
- Will the salesperson ask for referrals from current clients and prospects?
- Will the salesperson effectively use the phone to sell or for prospecting?
- Will the salesperson be coachable and does he follow instructions without change or modification?

How Can You as the Manager Tell if Your Veteran Salesperson Has Sales Call Reluctance®?

More than 25 years of pioneering research by world-renowned behavioral scientists, George W. Dudley and Shannon L. Goodson, have shown that sales people typically manifest this sales call reluctance® fear in one of twelve avoidance behaviors. Sales people avoid following through on sales (or even initiating that first contact) by diverting themselves into unproductive activities.

Observable Behaviors of Sales Call Reluctance® in Veteran Salespeople	Yes or No
You see the salesperson constantly worrying and less likely to take social risks.	
You see the salesperson over-analyzing and under-act in prospecting.	
You see the salesperson obsessed with image.	
You see the salesperson fearful of making group presentation.	
You see the salesperson ashamed of sales career.	
You see the salesperson fearful of intruding on others.	
You see the salesperson intimidated by up-market clientele.	
You see the salesperson fearful of loss of friends.	
You see the salesperson fearful of loss of family approval.	
You see the salesperson fearful of disturbing existing business or client relationships.	
You see the salesperson fear using the telephone for prospecting or self-promotional purposes.	
You see the salesperson rebuffs attempts to be coached.	

Results and Benefits:

- Use the Sales Call Reluctance® assessment to screen new sales candidates. Use it as a diagnostic tool to make sure you have the best sales candidate before hiring. Some candidates might come with glowing references and have excellent sales skills but might have tremendous emotional fears to stop them from building a profitable clientele base.

- Use the Sales Call Reluctance® assessment as a diagnostic tool to help veteran sales professionals overcome any emotional barriers limiting the person to having an outstanding sales career.

- The **SPQ GOLD® Sales Call Reluctance®** assessment does not measure intelligence, technical knowledge, self-presentation, and appearance. Nor does it check references. All those issues remain quite important and the hiring manager still needs to verify all these components. **SPQ GOLD® Sales Call Reluctance®** does uncover what could have been hidden from view even in a fairly comprehensive series of interviews.

- Most salespeople during the interview process, will tend to exaggerate their sales abilities, so be diligent about checking references.

Chapter 11

Recommended Profiles

Recommended Profile for Administrative Assistant – No Sales:

DISC Profile:

We recommend hiring an administrative assistant with no sales responsibilities, who has a blend of two behavioral styles, **High Steady** and **High Cautious** (with a score 50 or higher).

The strengths of a person with Steady behavior style will bring to the position a sense of customer service, patience to do routine tasks, and desire to be part of a team. The strengths of a person with Cautious behavior style will bring to the position a sense of organization, follow through with high standards, and an eye for detailed paperwork

Motivators, Personal Values, and Attitudes Profile:

We recommend hiring an administrative assistant with a **high Money-motivation score.** A Money-motivated person responds to money concepts such as bonus, salary, and commissions. This person is very practical about maximizing his/her effort, time, money, and resources to get the most value from the situation. Another motivator that is a good compliment to **Money** is **Learning** or **Altruism**. A Learning-motivated person enjoys learning new ideas and can be an asset within industries where best practices are constantly evolving and the employer can fuel an employee's natural desire to learn and reap the benefits of receiving up to date professional knowledge. An Altruism-motivated person loves to help people in need and this natural service-oriented passion can bring joy and warmth to all client and inter-office relationships.

We prefer employers to not hire an administrative assistant with a high Political/Power-motivation score. A Political/Power-motivated person desires power and/or leadership, and has a strong desire to lead, direct and control own destiny. This is a person looking for advancement of position in life and influence over others. In other words, such a person might not be satisfied by remaining an administrative assistant. Perhaps a long-term goal is the desire to be the owner of the company or to be a high ranking manager within the profession.

If there is no room for career advancement present within your organization to go beyond being an administrative assistant, the Political/Power-motivated person will feel dissatisfaction due to lack of advancement opportunities and ultimately leave your organization.

Another possibility is that you might be training your own competition as the Political/Power-motivated person might want to use your organization as a stepping stone to fulfill a greater career goal. As a manager, it is recommended that you hire a person who is motivated and satisfied having a career as an administrative assistant, not to hire and train your future competition.

Axiology Based Profile:

We recommend hiring an administrative assistant with a high score in all areas listed below:

- ☑ How well a person feels and understands people with compassion and empathy
- ☑ How well a person thinks and can make sound decisions
- ☑ How well a person relates to and acts in real, concrete terms
- ☑ How a person relates to rules, procedures and structure. Does the person understand there are rules in life or not? We want to make sure the person does <u>not</u> have a **maverick quality**
- ☑ How well does a person understand his own ability? How much self-confidence does a person have in his own abilities?
- ☑ How well a person understands what to do in a job situation
- ☑ How confident the person is in his own ability to reach future goals

An axiology based assessment tool can determine a person's capacity on "soft skills" such as empathy, leadership, making decisions, confidence, etc. that is very critical to job performance. If the "soft skill" talent has been developed by the person and is necessary for the job, the person will be very effective. If job performance is lower than desired for a current employee, it could be that the talent or "soft skills" has not been developed fully, and you, the employer have an opportunity to develop and ultimately retain top talent by providing job training on specific "soft skills" critical to superior job performance.

Recommended Profile for Sales Position:
BSRP Inc.'s SPQ Gold™ Sales Call Reluctance Profile:

It is highly recommended that all potential sales candidates take the **"SPQ Gold® Sales Call Reluctance"** assessment by Behavioral Sciences Research Press Inc. (BSRP) of Dallas, TX, to see if the candidate has any hesitation such as making calls, making contacts, following up with prospects, yielding to prospects/clients or asking for referrals, etc prior to being hired.

There are a total of twelve forms of call reluctance® measured on the assessment. The report also measures a person's ability to be coached. **The diagnostic results gained from this report is far more important than knowing the person's behavior style. You can have a great sales person with a great personality but if the person has a severe case of call reluctance®, that person will not be effective in prospecting and perhaps affect sales production.**

Reminder: The purpose of the *SPQ GOLD® Sales Call Reluctance assessment* is to measure how likely a person will prospect. It does <u>uncover</u> what could have been <u>hidden</u> from view even in a fairly comprehensive series of interviews.

DISC Profile:

In general, we recommend hiring for a sales position, someone who has at least one behavior style High Influential (with a score 50 or higher). The strengths of an Influential person means the person can come across more friendly, and usually build relationship quickly that is persuasive, and people-oriented.

Depending on the sales industry, a complementary behavior style that can blend well with the High Influential is the High Dominant, High Steady or High Cautious.

A blend of High Dominant behavior style can bring elements of being driven and having a "make it happen attitude" with speed and high results orientation. A blend of Steady behavior style can bring elements of customer-service and patience to the style. A blend of High Cautious behavior style can bring elements of efficiency and attention to complex information with follow-through.

Motivators, Personal Values, and Attitudes Profile:

For a sales position, we recommend hiring a person with a **high Money-motivation score**. A Money-motivated person responds to money concepts such as bonus, salary and commissions. This person is very practical about maximizing his/her effort, time, money, and resources to get the most value from the situation.

Another motivator that is a good complement to **Money** is **Learning** or **Altruism**. A Learning-motivated person enjoys learning new ideas and can be an asset within industries where best practices are constantly evolving and the employer can fuel an employee's natural desire to learn and reap the benefits of receiving up to date professional knowledge.

An Altruism-motivated person loves to help people in need and this natural service-oriented passion can bring joy and warmth to all client and inter-office relationships. **In general, we recommend employers use extreme caution in hiring a sales person with a high Political/Power-motivation score.**

A Political/Power-motivated person desires power and/or leadership, and has a strong desire to lead, direct and control own destiny. This is a person looking for advancement of position in life and to influence over others. In other words, such a person might not be satisfied by remaining as a regular sales person; the person might be motivated to become a senior sales leader, national sales trainer, go to the senior management level, or move to the executive level. Perhaps there is a desire to be the owner of the company or be a high ranking manager within the profession.

If there is no room for career advancement present within your organization to go beyond being a sales person, the Political/Power-motivated person will eventually feel dissatisfaction due to lack of advancement opportunities and ultimately leave your organization.

Another possibility is that you might be training your own competition as the Political/Power-motivated person might want to use your organization as a stepping stone to fulfill a great career goal. However, if you are a manager/owner within a large company/organization and have room for advancement (i.e. branch manager, senior sales, vice president of sales etc.) then you might consider hiring the person with a high Political/Power-motivation score.

Remember, a Political/Power-motivated person desires control of their own destiny and if you as the manager can't provide or fulfill the "carrot or golden ring" to your sales person, then the person will most likely leave for greener pastures. As a manager, it is recommended that you hire a person who is motivated and satisfied having a long sustaining career as a sales person, not to hire and train your future competition.

Axiology Based Profile:

We recommend hiring a sales person with a high score in all areas listed below:

- ☑ How well a person feels and understands people with compassion and empathy
- ☑ How well a person thinks and can make decisions soundly
- ☑ How well a person relates to and does acts in real, concrete terms
- ☑ How a person relates to rules, procedures and structure.
- ☑ Does the person understand or not that there are rules in life?
- ☑ Does the person have the ability to think outside the box in a sales situation and come up with creative solutions to difficult challenges?
- ☑ Does the person display a sense of being a **maverick**?
- ☑ How well a person understands own abilities

- ☑ How much self-confidence does a person have in own abilities?
- ☑ How well a person understands what to do in a job situation
- ☑ How confident the person is in his own ability to reach future goals

An axiology based assessment tool can determine a person's capacity on "soft skills" such as empathy, leadership, making decisions, confidence, etc. that is very critical to job performance. If the "soft skill" talent has been developed by the person and is necessary for the job, the person will be very effective. If job performance is lower than desired for a current employee, it could be that the talent or "soft skills" has not been developed fully, and you, the employer, have an opportunity to develop and ultimately retain top talent by providing job training on specific "soft skills" critical to superior job performance.

Exception: Many top performers can have high scores in all areas but still have a low self-esteem score. This might be because they love to keep improving.

Chapter 12

Before You Hire

B *efore you hire, you need a do a* **Job Analysis** *to understand the job being filled. Then you can create your* **Job Description** *which explains how the job fits within the organization/company. This will lead you in creating the* **Job Contract** *that your hire will sign agreeing to fulfill the job duties. The Job Contract will also serve as an important and highly versatile management tool for professional training and career development for your new employee.*

Outline on How to do a Job Analysis

Understand the job being filled by putting yourself in the job itself. If you're having trouble, one good way to get information for a job analysis is to talk to successful employees and supervisors at other companies that have similar positions.

- What kind of behavior style, values, soft skills, education, experience, etc. are needed to do the job to your level of satisfaction?

- What are the mental/physical tasks involved (ranging from judging, planning and managing to cleaning, lifting and welding)
- How the job will be done (the methods and equipment to be used)
- The reason the job exists (including an explanation of job goals and how they relate to other positions in the company)
- The qualifications needed (training, knowledge, skills and personality traits)

Outline on How to Create a Job Description & Specification

Use the job analysis to write a job description and a job specification. The same information gained from the process will also allow you to create your recruitment materials, such as a classified advertisement (see Chapter 13).

The **job description** is basically an outline of how the job fits in to the company. As a hiring tool, a job description is a written description identifying a job by title, essential functions and requirements. A well-crafted job description also spells out the knowledge, abilities and skills required to perform a job successfully. It should point out in broad terms the job's goals, responsibilities, and duties. The **job specification** describes the personal requirements you expect from the employee. It can list any educational requirements, desired experience and specialized skills, or knowledge required.

For a one-person business hiring its first employee, these steps might seem unnecessary, but remember, you are laying the foundations for your personnel policy, which will be essential as your company grows. Keeping detailed records from the time you hire your first employee will make things a lot easier when you hire your fiftieth.

Suggested information to be included in a **Job Description and Job Specification:**

- What is the job title?
- Whom does the person report to?
- Develop a job statement or summary describing the position's major and minor duties
- What is the position in detail? What is the person going to do precisely in terms of activities?
- What are the goals of the job?
- What are the responsibilities/accountabilities of the employee?
- What are the duties?
- What are the expectations?
- Define how the job relates to other positions in the company/ organization
- Define which jobs are subordinate and which jobs are of equal responsibility and authority
- Where the person is going to be doing it – office, off-site or home?
- Is the position permanent, temporary, contract, part-time or full-time?
- The goals for the position such as expectations, minimum quotas.
- Reasons for termination.
- How to get promoted.
- How long you expect person to remain in the position as a minimum amount of time?
- What are the minimal educational requirements, GED, BS, MBA etc?
- Do they need to have any prior work-related experience to bring to the job?
- Do they need any specialized skills, knowledge, license, certification required for the job? List any physical or

other special requirements associated with the job, and any occupational hazards

- Salary range, benefits, compensation plan, bonus, vacation days, sick days, insurance, etc.
- What is your company/organization's philosophy/mission statement? Why your company does the things it does? How is your company unique?

Employment Preferences

Another aid in hiring is to provide the candidate a listing of employment preferences. The answers can be quite enlightening when studied with the responses to interview questions (see Chapter 14) and a review of an application form. The answers to these questions are important regardless of the level of the position that you are seeking to fill. For example, if the candidate ranks job security as number 1 and the company is facing some challenges then could lead to a possibility of a misfit of values and preferences.

Here is a sample employment preferences questionnaire:

Rank the factors listed below, on a scale of 1 through 10, with 10 being the most important and 1 being the least important to you in considering a position with our company.

___ 401(k) plan
___ Health and dental insurance
___ Incentive bonus plan
___ Initial base compensation
___ Job security
___ Opportunity for advancement
___ Retirement plan
___ Vacation time
___ Working conditions
___ Working hours

You can use the Job Description and make it into a Job Contract where the new employee will sign and date it as a contract and as a promise to meet the standards you hired your new employee for. The supervising manager should also sign and date the Job Contract as an agreement to hold the new employee accountable to what is written in the contract and it can become an excellent management tool for **professional training** and **career development** for the new hire.

Keys to Creating Job Descriptions

- Flexibility is the key in job—there is always more than one way to achieve the same results
- Create more generic job descriptions that emphasize **expectations** and **accountabilities**, rather than specific tasks
- Encouraging employees to focus on results rather than job duties
- Having a more wide-ranging job description is also easier to maintain--it doesn't require modification with every minor change in duties

What does an assessment specialist needs from an employer/ manager before he can help?

- Detailed Job description
- Profile/assessments of the manager and other team members
- Reasons why this position needs to be filled
- Any notes from resumes and interview
- Visual organization chart
- Any other information that will help the specialist know more about the organization and team which might influence the decision making process

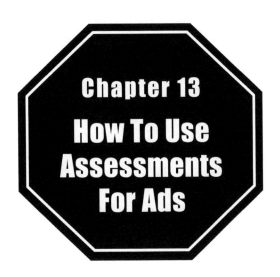

Chapter 13

How To Use Assessments For Ads

In this chapter you can see how to design ads using behaviors and motivators

Steps:

1. Look at the job description. Pick the words that would emphasize the behavioral style of desired employee. This would include words like: enthusiastic, people-oriented, bottom-line communicator, etc.

2. Motivators: Use words like money-motivated, customer service-oriented, learning opportunities, harmonious work environment, etc

3. Axiology-based: High empathy towards customers, respect for boundaries, and practical common sense

So how would these ads look?

1. Administrative Assistant:

As mentioned before, the person is likely to be more introverted and focused on follow through.

The descriptors might be:

- Cautious
- Detailed
- Loyal
- Consistent
- Analytical

2 of top 3 motivators might be:

☑ Business-environment

☑ Customer-service focused

☑ Opportunities to learn

2. Sales Assistant:

As mentioned before, the person is likely to be people-oriented. The descriptors might be:

- Enthusiastic
- Friendly
- People-oriented
- Steady

2 of top 3 motivators are:

☑ Money-motivated

☑ Customer-service oriented

To put together these ads, all you have to do is pick words which reflect these behaviors and motivators along with specific skills and experience you expect them to have.

Job Advertisement Checklist

Below is a list of suggested information to be included in the layout of an effective job advertisement. The list is loosely structured in order and this is in no way prescriptive—use a sequence that works best. The bold items are those which would normally be essential; the others are optional depending on local policy and circumstances.

- ☑ **Job Title.**
- ☑ **Employer (if possible)**
- ☑ **Job Base Location**
- ☑ **Succinct description of business/organization/division activity and market position and aims**
- ☑ **To whom the position reports – or indicate where the role is in the structure (entry level, managerial, executive level)**
- ☑ **Outline of job role and purpose**
- ☑ **Candidate Profile: Indicate qualifications, experience required, scale and size of responsibilities, and territory of role outline etc. of ideal candidate**
- ☑ **Indicate salary or salary guide**
- ☑ Indicate if position is full-time, or permanent or a short-term contract
- ☑ Indicate package details or guide (pension, car etc)
- ☑ Explanation of recruitment process
- ☑ **Response and Application Instructions**
- ☑ **Contact details as necessary such as address, phone, fax, email, etc.**
- ☑ Job and or Advertisement reference code (Advertisement references help you analyze results from different Advertisements for the same job)
- ☑ Corporate Branding and company website address
- ☑ Quality accreditations, i.e. CFP, RN, PhD.
- ☑ Compliance with U.S. Equal Employment Opportunity Commission (EEOC) Guidelines

Chapter 14

Interviewing

How effective is interviewing in most companies? According to research by Michigan State University, the typical interviewing process used at most companies is, at best, only **14%** effective in predicting successful hires. The remaining 86% keeps you extremely busy managing the revolving door of resumes, applications, hires, and fires.

In turn, your profits suffer from lapses in staff coverage that equate to lost opportunities, erosion of customer satisfaction, continual training expenses, and seriously wasted time for management.

Common Mistakes in Interviewing:

☑ As we have mentioned before, most managers are not trained in hiring. Most of them don't know how to prepare for the interview. We recommend having a list of questions to make sure that you cover the essential components of the job.

☑ Most managers and sales professionals are people-oriented

and hence are more impressed by the "personality" of the candidate than the credentials and ability to perform the job. Some candidates do a great job of being persuasive.

- ☑ Another problem in interviews is the desire of the manager to dominate the speaking and sell the job to the candidate.
- ☑ Quite often the focus is more on how the manager feels about the candidate than what data he is collecting during the interview. Your gut feel is important, but it is not the only determinant of the desirability of the candidate.
- ☑ Sometime a manager does not have an accurate job description. The manager has not written a list of behaviors, attitudes, and motivators that are necessary and critical to the success in job performance.
- ☑ Most managers have not created a list of desired behaviors especially the soft skills (see chapter on axiology) for each position such as attention to detail, teamwork, leadership, control, initiative etc.

One of our clients was interested in a candidate so we evaluated the person. We felt that there was a good chance that this person could fit the role. During the conversation, the client revealed that she had come across another individual that she felt should be evaluated as well. We dug deeper and found that the reason for evaluating the second candidate was that during the interview, the manager liked the candidate, but the candidate was not very forthcoming with details.

She thought the candidate was possibly shy and did not feel comfortable talking about himself. So the client concluded that if we provided our battery of assessments, we could learn more about the applicant and she could make a better hiring decision. On the surface it seems logical.

But here was our concern. If the person was not expressing himself well in the interview, why should she put this person in front of her clients?

The light bulb went on and she immediately realized that her curiosity was her driving force. She should have focused on how the person presented himself and whether he would be compctent and skilled in interacting with her clients. The client realized that the person had already demonstrated to her that he would not be suitable as a customer service person, so there was no need to provide any assessments to this candidate.

Our focus is not to sell assessments but to function in the role of teaching managers to be better managers. *Hearing what is not directly said in the interview is a critical skill.*

The three keys to interviewing:

a. Interview for the job and not the person.

At every moment of the interview, your focus needs to be on evaluating the candidate for the job. It is easy to get sidetracked by how the candidate presents himself and fail to connect the answers to the job. Some managers do not even have any questions in advance.

b. Listen to the said and unsaid. Salespeople have a challenge in listening to people who are not prospects. The salesperson has his antenna up when the prospect gives any buying signals yet the same salesperson fails to notice discrepancies between the written data and the verbal data provided by the candidate during the hiring process.

The simplest thing to do is to take notes during the interview. It is an excellent idea to formulate questions based on the person's resume and the job description and focus more on eliciting answers to those questions than talking. Dig deep without being obnoxious.

If possible, have a second person in the room during the interview to lend a helping ear on the verbal communication and careful eye on the non-verbal communication/body language while you take notes.

c. Confirm your information based on the resume and
other references during the interview. Make sure you address
any discrepancy between their resume and interview. This step
is about getting reliable information. Ask for examples and
clarification.

Check three references; two of the references should be
professional and one should be personal to endorse the character
of the candidate. Be sure to keep your questions as objective as
possible. If you're speaking to the professional references, make
sure they relate directly to the candidate's job performance and
duties and to information provided on the application or resume,
or to information provided during the interview.

Forms of discrimination that apply to interviewing and hiring
are also applicable to reference checking, so be sure to avoid
questions that involve race, age, disabilities, national origin,
religion, or marital status. For a personal reference, find out how
long they've known the person and then ask about the person's
character and work ethic; you might also ask if the person would
hire the applicant themselves, if they had an appropriate job
opening to fill.

One of the key predictors about the candidate's performance
at your job could be their past performance. We recommend
asking questions about why a candidate is leaving his or her
current position. This is very important. Don't just gloss over this
question. Whatever prompted the person to leave the job could re-
occur in your work environment as well.

Conducting the Face-To-Face Interview in Two Parts
Part One: General Interview Questions

As the manager, the bottom line purpose of conducting a

general interview question is to determine:

- What can the candidate add to my enterprise/company/ organization as an employee and can the candidate prove it to me?
- Why does the candidate want a position in my company/ organization?

Asking good interview questions will allow you to gain specific information and insight about the candidate's;

> *Capabilities*
>
> *Attitudes*
>
> *Values*
>
> *Motivational Driving Force*
>
> *Thought processes (thinking abilities)*
>
> *Self awareness*

The best method is to **ask open-ended interview** questions and let the candidate's answers reveal the qualities mentioned above.

An example of an open question, "how would you describe the following four terms: success, achievement, challenge, and growth?" At face value, they might seem silly and too obvious but as a manager, press the candidate to give you good, thoughtful specific answer that shows the person has abilities to be self-reflective, can think and yet be realistic. If the answer is too general and not specific such as, "I want to grow" then ask the candidate to explain and elaborate further with a comment such as, "What do you mean by grow?"

While conducting the interviewing process, don't settle for "glib" answers to important open-ended questions such as "Where do you see yourself in 5 years?" The purpose of the question is meant to be thought-provoking.

As the employer, you want to see the thinking process taking place on how the candidate arrived at the answer. If the candidate is afraid to pause and reflect during the interview process, even stumble and bumble as the person wrestles with the question, what confidence do you as the employer have that the candidate will be open and reflective on the job? Confident candidates should be open and reflective otherwise you are headed towards possibly hiring un-trainable employees who can't think own their own two feet.

Part Two: Behavioral Interviewing Questions

The method of Behavioral Interviewing has been around since the 1970's when industrial psychologists wanted to developed a process to predict whether an employee would succeed at the job. Large organizations such as AT&T and Accenture (the former Andersen Consulting) have been using this process for years.

The foundation behind behavioral interviewing is that if candidates were asked question about past behaviors/ performance, it would be an accurate predictor of future performance in similar situations. Behavioral interviewing is said to be 55% predictive of future-on-the-job behavior while traditional interviewing is only 10-14% percent predictive.

This is why it is extremely critical as a manager/employer to understand the job position thoroughly. You have to understand the behavior style, the motivators and the soft skills (axiology) needed for an employee to do a job successfully *before you even begin* your hiring process and evaluate candidates.

Now that you have the job description already written, you can create behavioral based interview questions to support your decision whether or not to hire a candidate.

For example, an administrative assistant requires having the performance behaviors such as attention to detail, customer-oriented, etc. By asking good questions, it will be easier to determine does the candidate have these qualities? Does the candidate have the potential to be successful based on job-related experiences, behaviors, knowledge, skills, and abilities that have been decided are desirable in a particular position?

As the manager, the bottom line purpose of conducting a **behavioral interview question** process is to determine:

    a) What the candidate did in a previous job that is similar to the current job situation?

    b) How the candidate solved the similar situation?

    c) What process and skill sets did the candidate use to solve the situation?

Basically, if the candidate was able to perform the job well in the past, then the candidate should be able to perform it well again!

What is the difference between an open-ended general interview question and a behavioral interview question?

The open-ended general question usually seeks a general answer while the behavioral interview question will be highly specific.

Here is an example of a behavioral interview question: "Describe a situation that required a number of things to be done at the same time. How did you handle it? What was the result?" The vital word is "time" and the answer requires a "specific result" in a "specific situation."

A question such as "What would you do if you have a problem to solve?" allows candidates to tap into their imagination to answer and is an open-ended type question. The word, "if" is the clue word that indicates that this is a "how a candidate thinks" type of question. This question does not require a past experience example. Asking situational questions such as "How would you handle XYZ situation?" does not reveal how much accountability a candidate brings to the situation; in fact, it could be minimal.

Asking candidates behavioral interview questions requires the person to be highly and thoroughly prepared for the interview. It is nearly impossible to prepare "canned" answers to these questions because of the vast number and variety of questions compared with the open-ended interview questions. With open-ended questions, there is always a possibly that the candidate will tell you what you want to hear or "make up stuff." With behavioral interview questions and with careful listening skills, it's much more difficult to give responses that are untrue to the candidate's character or to "make up stuff."

By looking at the candidate's resume, you can ask specific behavioral interview questions. For example, on the resume, the candidate claims to be "organized." A natural behavioral question for the interviewer would be: "Tell me about a time when you organized a project?" Now the candidate should offer a satisfactory explanations or story about his/her success when organizing a project or event.

What to look for in the answers while conducting a behavioral interview

A good candidate will give the answer in a succinct story format filled with details, and filled with action verbs that are hopefully interesting and memorable. You should evaluate the quality of the answers to your behavioral questions based on three crucial elements:

    a) The beginning of the story — "There was a **time/situation/ task or problem....**"

    b) The middle of the story — "The **action** steps I took...."

    c) The end of the story — "The **end result or outcome** was...."

Some people refer to this response process as **STAR** (Situation, Task, Action and Result) or **SAR** (Situation, Action and Result) Technique.

Situation or Task	Did the candidate describe a specific event or situation that needed to be accomplished? This situation can be from a previous job, from a volunteer experience, or any relevant event.
Action candidate took	What actions did the candidate take? If candidate discussed a group project or effort, did candidate describe what he/she did – not the efforts of the team?
Results candidate achieved	What happened? How did the event end? What did the candidate accomplish? What did the candidate learn?

The candidate's answers to your behavioral questions should reveal if the candidate has the desired characteristics you are seeking especially the "soft skills" such as "critical thinker, self-starter, attention to detail, empathy, teamwork" etc.

Ask **probing questions** while interviewing. Listen carefully to the candidate's story/answer to listen for the specific behavioral traits you are looking for in the candidate. You can probe for more depth or detail such as "What were you thinking at that point?" or "Tell me more about your meeting with that person," or "Lead me through your decision process." If the candidate told a story that's anything but totally honest, their response will not hold up through the barrage of probing questions.

As a manager/employer, you can ask behavioral interview questions that are framed as statements that typically start out: "Tell about a time...." or "Describe a situation...." For example, the desired behavioral trait is teamwork, the statement you can ask the candidate is "Describe a situation where others you were working with on a project disagreed with your ideas. What did you do?"

You can ask candidates behavioral interview questions to determine how they react in a negative situation. Hopefully, candidates will share their negative experiences and how they cope or better yet, how they still created positive outcomes.

How to evaluate the candidate's answers to your behavioral questions?

You can create a simple evaluation system by creating a worksheet with three columns: Column 1 has your list of your behavioral questions; Column 2 has space for you to write your notes about your candidate's answers; and in Column 3 use a simple 1-5 rating system to grade the quality of the candidate's answer based on your criteria.

Simple Ranking System for Candidates Answers to Behavioral Questions

5. MUCH MORE THAN ACCEPTABLE: Significantly above criteria required for successful job performance

4. MORE THAN ACCEPTABLE: Generally exceeds criteria relative to quality and quantity of behavior required.

3. ACCEPTABLE: Meets criteria relative to quality and quantity of behavior required.

2. LESS THAN ACCEPTABLE: Generally does not meet criteria relative to quality and quantity of behavior required.

1. MUCH LESS THAN ACCEPTABLE: Significantly below criteria required for successful job performance.

Sample Candidate's Story/Response to Behavioral Interview Question:

Situation (S):

Advertising revenue was falling off for my local newspaper, the Citrus Chronicle, and large numbers of long-term advertisers were not renewing contracts.

Action (A):

I designed a new promotional packet to go with the rate sheet and compared the benefits of Citrus Chronicle circulation with other ad media in the area to contact former clients. I also set-up a joint venture with the Citrus Chamber of Commerce to offer a special promotion to current and new Chamber members who have never placed ads with the Chronicle.

Result (R):

We signed contracts with 15 former advertisers for daily ads and five for special supplements. We increased our new advertisers by 20 percent over the same period last year.

See Appendix 1 for Sample List of Performance Skills/ Behavior with Behavioral Interview Questions and Evaluation Rating System

For the Employer:
What qualities are you looking for in the answer?

Why are you leaving your current job?
Or
Why did you leave your last job?

1. To identify past problems a candidate might carry over into new job.
2. Candidate gives a positive reason for joining and leaving a company.
3. Candidate sees new position as an important step forward in career.

Why should we employ you rather than one of the other candidates?

1. Candidate is able to distinguish himself from others highlighting unique qualities that is best for the job.
2. Candidate has researched the company thoroughly and studied the job description.
3. Candidate is able to demonstrate clearly how skills, qualifications, and accomplishments match the employer's specific needs.
4. Candidate is able to convey genuine enthusiasm for the position.

What are your strengths and weaknesses?
How do you take advantage of them?
(Advance/Thought Provoking)

1. Listen for quality of answer.
2. Look for evidence of critical self-assessment and a commitment to continuous self-development.
3. Candidate shows specific job-related strengths and accomplishments.
4. Candidate identifies one weakness that could be viewed both as positive and negative, e.g. candidate is a perfectionist who tends to work too many long hours.
5. Listen for how candidate was successful in addressing a weakness tendency.

"What Are Your Major Weaknesses?"
What have you done to overcome them?"
(Advance/Thought Provoking)

1. Listen for candidate's self awareness of own abilities and explains about a weakness or a challenge the person had to overcome.
2. Listen for candidate's awareness of weakness which could have an impact on others and how candidate was able to overcome that. Listen for how sensitive candidate is to other's feelings.

Ex. A slow worker can affect the project for someone else on a deadline.

3. Listen for candidate's self development in an area that is challenging and how person has grown from that experience.
4. If candidate denies having a weakness or does not admit to having one, this could be a sign of not being coachable or being too arrogant to be managed.

Tell me about yourself

1. Find out how well suited candidate is to the job.
2. Find out how candidate can benefit the company/ organization.
3. Candidate spends no longer than two minutes answering this question.
4. Listen for candidate's ability to carry out detailed company research in analyzing the job description in advance.
5. Listen for candidate's skills, qualifications, and accomplishments that relate to the advertised position.
6. See if candidate is able to offer a good solution to your managerial problem (i.e. increase sales, retain current clients, etc.) better than anyone else

Where do you see yourself in five years' time?

1. This question is to determine candidate's career plan
2. Does candidate have well planned short-term and long-term career goals? Is the job position consistent with these goals?
3. If candidate is hired, how likely will the candidate commit himself fully to the company or will candidate seize the first opportunity to move on?
4. Was candidate able to demonstrate a structured way of establishing goals?
5. Is the candidate seeking promotion within the organization as part of career progression?
6. Does the candidate appear to be ambitious, yet realistic?
7. Do you hear the candidate has a plan to develop professionally within the company?

Why do you want to work for our company?

1. The interviewer is trying to discover how much you know about the company. Did the candidate do detailed company research?
2. Does the candidate display knowledge of the company and an awareness of the challenges it faces?
3. Has candidate researched about the company's organizational structure; its financial history; its range of products, goods or services; its aims and objectives; its philosophy and culture; its trading methods; its history, current position, and future developments; its competitors; its training programs; its attitude towards its customers; its achievements; and any problems it might have.
4. Does the candidate's answer meet and solve your organizational needs?

Describe a typical working day in your current/previous job.

1. Does the candidate "blame" others for mishap?
2. Does the candidate rely excessively on others to pull candidate through the situation?

Take me through your resume.
What are you most proud of on your resume?

1. Candidate shows self-reflective answers.
2. Candidate displays how candidate thinks and shows solid thinking processes.

How would you describe the following four terms: success, achievement, challenge, and growth?

1. Candidate shows self-reflective answers.
2. Candidate displays how candidate thinks and shows solid thinking processes.

Have you ever been fired from a job?

1.   Does the candidate "blame" others for firing?

What skills do you enjoy using most and why?

1. Is the candidate aware of abilities?
2. Is the candidate working to improve self?

How did you do on your last performance appraisal? What were the key strengths and weakness pointed out by your supervisor?

1. Does the candidate "blame" others for poor performance?
2. Does the candidate rely excessively on others to pull candidate through the situation?

What is the biggest mistake you've made in your career? What steps have you taken to ensure it does not happen again?

1. Does the candidate "blame" others for mistake?
2. Does the candidate excessively seek others to help him/her get through the situation?

Have you ever worked in an environment similar to this one? Please describe the similarities and the differences?

1. Listen for how the candidate likes to be managed
2. How does the candidate's style match your managerial style?
3. Listen for how the job fits with the candidate's strengths and job preference

Are you familiar with the corporate culture here?
How do you think you will fit in here?

1.   Listen for how the candidate likes to be managed.

What would be the ideal way you would
envision spending your first day here?

1. Listen for how the candidate likes to be managed.
2. How does the candidate's learning style match your
   teaching style?

What were the worst working conditions you ever
experienced? How did you handle them?

1. Listen for how the candidate likes to be managed.
2. How does the candidate's style match your managerial
   style?

What contributed to the best working
conditions you had ever experienced?

1. Listen for how the candidate likes to be managed.
2. How does the candidate's style match your managerial
   style?

What types of work do you like?
Routine task, projects, or troubleshooting?

1. Listen for how the candidate likes to be managed. Does it
   match your managerial style?
2. Listen for how the job fits with the candidate's strengths
   and job preference.

Do you consider yourself more task-oriented or project-oriented?

1. Listen and check how well the candidate's preference matches with the job description.
2. A task-oriented person usually requires more managerial supervision.
3. A project-oriented person usually requires less managerial supervision.

Describe your work ethics with examples.

1. Listen for how the candidate likes to be managed.
2. Do the candidate's ethics meet and match the job requirement?
3. Listen for how the job fits with the candidate's strengths and job preference.

Tell me about the best boss you ever had. What made him/her so great to work for?

1. Listen for how the candidate likes to be managed.
2. How does the candidate's preference match your managerial style?

Tell me about the worst boss you ever had. What made him/her so difficult to work for?

1. Listen for how the candidate likes to be managed.
2. How does the candidate's preference match your managerial style?

How does your boss get you to do your best work?

1. Listen for how the candidate likes to be managed.
2. Listen for the candidate's motivators and values.

What do you feel an employer owes to his employees?
What do you feel an employee owes to his employer?

1. Listen for the candidate's motivators and values.
2. Listen; does the candidate value, practicality, money, customer service, teamwork and efficiency?

If you started working for us tomorrow,
what could you contribute immediately?

1. Listen for the candidate's motivator and values.
2. Can the candidate solve your problem?

If you are offered this position, how much notice
will you have to give to your current employer?

1. Listen for the candidate's motivator and values.
2. Does the candidate show respect to current employer?

How would your co-workers describe you?

1. Do the candidate's behaviors fit with your job description?

Did you ever have to deal with a co-worker who was not
pulling his/her own weight? What did you do about it?

1. Does the candidate appear to be confrontational?
2. Does the candidate appear to be diplomatic in solving the situation?

How would you respond to a co-worker who suggests an
improvement that you know would not work?

1. Does the candidate appear to be confrontational?
2. Does the candidate appear to be diplomatic in solving the situation?

How do you handle breaks in routine, interruptions and last minute changes?

1. Does the candidate's behavior and preference fit well with the job description?

Tell me about a time you became frustrated or flustered because of job pressures? How did you handle it?

1. Does the candidate have resilience to overcome normal challenges?
2. Does the candidate have good coping with stress strategies and can relay on self rather than others to solve the situation?

If you could attend a class or seminar, what would the topic be and why?

1. Listen for the candidate's motivator and values.

Have you ever been passed over for a promotion for which you felt you most qualified? What did you do about it?

1. Listen for the candidate's motivator and values.
2. Is the candidate looking for upward mobility within a company?

What aspect of this job as I have described it appeals to you the most? The least?

1. Listen for the candidate's natural enjoyment of using his/her personal talents to get the job completed. Does the talent match the job description?
2. Listen for the candidate's least favorite aspects of the job—is it critical/necessary for getting the job completed?

What will you do if you don't get this position?

1. Does the candidate's self esteem appear to be solid or less confident?
2. Does the candidate appear to be survival mode?

Why should I hire you?

1. Does the candidate's self esteem appear to be solid or less confident?
2. Does the candidate's past performance matches closely with your company's present needs?

See Appendix 2 for partial list of Interview Questions Specific for Administrative Assistant, Receptionist, Marketing Specialist, and Salesperson.

See Appendix 3 for a Candidate Interview Checklist, a graphic organization to help hiring manager stay on track and remain consistent when interviewing one or multiple candidates for a position.

Chapter 15

First 90 Days – Helping Your New Hire Succeed

The five keys to getting the most out of a new employee in the first 90 days are:

❶ Enthusiastic welcome

❷ Clear, written expectations and consequences

❸ Detailed plan for orientation and training

❹ Structure and support from the manager and the team

❺ Supervision and feedback

Everybody wants to feel that he made the right decision when he took on a new job. Unfortunately, in a busy environment, the manager is keen to get the new employee to be productive from day one. A typical manager is busy putting out fires and is very rarely available to provide the support needed by a new team member.

Getting an employee to be productive is not always easy because the employee has a lot to learn about the new work environment. Therefore, how the manager introduces the work and the rest of the team to the new hire will determine how quickly the new employee will become assimilated and succeed in the organization. Let us go over each of the steps a manager needs to do to facilitate the quick success of the new hire.

Welcome Employees Enthusiastically

Make employees feel welcomed, wanted, and needed. Numerous studies have shown that relationships formed at work often determine whether an employee stays or leaves.

Build a Sense of Team

The landmark Gallup Poll book **"First Break All the Rules: What Great Managers do Differently,"** by Marcus Buckingham and Curt Coffman (Simon & Schuster, 1999), clearly emphasizes the fact that the relationship of an employee with his supervisor creates loyalty. So how do you build that sense of loyalty?

Here are some simple ideas that any manager can implement:

1. Greet all your employees with warmth.
2. Create an environment where people express pleasure in working with each other. An idea for fostering such an environment is writing thank you cards when somebody does a good job. Simply saying 'thank you' sincerely is always appreciated.
3. Make employee recognition and praise a public ritual.
4. Help people build bonds with each other so people feel part of a team. This can be accomplished by having regular team meetings, team building sessions, and special company or team events.
5. Let the employees know that you have high expectations for them because you firmly believe in their ability to succeed.

Create Clear Written Expectations and Consequences

This can be easily accomplished by having a detailed list of activities and outcomes that a person needs to perform. Using checklists like a weekly checklist can eliminate any ambiguity of what needs to be done. Simultaneously providing a detailed picture of the outcomes that are expected to be achieved will enhance a sense of mission and purpose within the team.

Quite often an employee might know what needs to be done, but might not have a clear sense of the consequences if he or she fails to perform the desired task. It is imperative to help the employee understand the consequences in two ways. First, let him see how his lack of activity or not reaching a goal will hurt the team and the company. Second, the employee must become aware that eventually all of this reflects on his work and will result in his being reprimanded or, ultimately, fired.

Sadly, this process of communicating expectations and consequences to the employee is missing from the orientation ritual of a number of companies. And those companies that do communicate expectations and consequences often do not follow through with the consequences.

Create and Execute a Detailed Plan for Orientation and Training

As mentioned before, busy managers find it difficult to give adequate time to help new employees learn and get acquainted with systems and other team members. Having a written plan in place can make it easier for the manager to implement this step. Also, creating some steps which can be done without direct supervision by the manager will free him to do important tasks during the training period.

Assess the Training Needs of the Employee

At this time the manager should assess the training needs of the new employee to perform the tasks. After you have explained the tasks and the desired outcomes, the manager must repeatedly communicate with the new employee as to what skills and resources will be required to make sure he can succeed at the job. The manager must be willing to listen closely because it is possible that the new hire might not feel comfortable or might not know what specifically he might end up needing.

Make sure that the training activities are broken up into their simplest form so that supervision is easy. Test the person's efficiency and effectiveness in doing the job. It is easy to explain a single task and then expect the person to perform that task without having a two-way dialog. This part is as much about listening and asking questions as much it is about telling.

Provide Ongoing Structure and Support from the Manager and the Team

We have mentioned this step separately though some managers include this in orientation and training. The employee must understand when and who to approach for clarification and support.

There are two reasons for this:

- One is that you do not want the employee to waste time and productivity trying to find out where to get the needed information and support. The employee might be stuck and might not seek help quickly either.

- The other reason is that you do not want the employee to keep interrupting you throughout your day. If you are not available or easily accessible, the employee might not know what action to take and the impact on productivity could impact your bottom line as well. A client's unanswered concern or unresolved problem could cause you to lose a client.

Provide Supervision and Feedback

This is another area to which most managers pay very little attention. Most managers have a "sink or swim" philosophy. It is critical to set a regular feedback time with a new employee. This could be done by e-mail, reports and in person. The new employee is eager to get praise, so it is important to interact with the new employee as often as the job allows.

In the beginning, the manager might help the new employee create the day's task list and check on the employee twice during the day. Make sure that the employee has all the resources needed and is proceeding in the manner you want.

This is the time for quick correction; do not wait to provide input. You want to point out the good and the bad as quickly as possible. Do not compromise on the standards or ignore sloppy work. You are reinforcing your expectations and nothing is more important than your actions.

If your operations/procedure manual asks for certain standards but you do not enforce them, you can easily expect for the standards to spiral down. Confront poor performance early. Hiring errors are inevitable. Be prepared to hold up that mirror. To care actually means to help the person know his strengths and weaknesses.

Recap of Actions for New Hire:
- Discuss and set 30-day, 60-day and 90-day goals for new hires.
- Meet with new hire daily for the first few weeks.
- As a welcoming gesture, organize a staff lunch on the employee's first day.
- Have the new hire shadow a co-worker.
- Have the new hire attend a staff meeting in every department to understand the big picture of how your company operates.
- Review the provided written procedures for repeated tasks.
- Cross-train your staff so new hires can get help if they find themselves in a pinch.

Make Use of your DISC Profile as a Manager

Using your DISC profile, let us see what your challenges could be:

D – Dominant/Director type managers delegate the tasks and wait for the results.

I - Expressive/Influential managers are more eager to please than to reprimand. Hence, they are more effusive in their praise and overly optimistic about people's ability to change and improve.

S - Steady/Amiable type managers might avoid conflict and might not bring up an issue until it is too late.

C - Cautious/Analytical type managers might micro-manage and focus more on procedures than results.

As mentioned before, confront poor performance early. In the understanding of talent, it frees the manager from blaming the employee. When you care about your business and your employee, you set the person up for success.

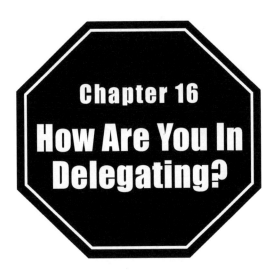

Chapter 16
How Are You In Delegating?

Directions: Answer "Yes" or "No" to each statement.

1. I have a clear visual flowchart for my team and everybody knows his/her roles on the team.
2. I know the best and highest use of my time and my role in the company, and the team flowchart reflects that.
3. I take time to provide the details to my team members and make sure they understand what their tasks are, why they are given, and by when they need to be completed.
4. I train my team members and provide the support they need with time, guidance, and resources to help them be successful in their roles.
5. I closely supervise my team members' authority and make sure they have adequate authority to go with their responsibilities.
6. My team members feel that they can approach me as soon as they feel that the tasks have unforeseen challenges or there are changes that need my input.
7. I hold meetings on a regular basis with my team members to monitor their progress and provide further guidance.

8. I make sure that my team members feel accountable for the results. Initially with new team members, I hold them accountable for activity and improving skills. For senior and experienced team members, I hold them accountable to results more often than activity and skills.

9. I have a reward system in place to assist and encourage team members.

10. My team members view delegation as an opportunity for growth and success.

Analyzing Your Answers: How Are You In Delegating?

If you answered "Yes" to seven or more: You are close to getting your team to do 75% or more of your work!

If you answered "No", find out what "No" means to each statement:

1. You rarely delegate or delegate without a systematic approach. You basically delegate whenever you are overwhelmed or don't want to be responsible for a task.

2. You are easily distracted and you are likely to be more active than productive. You have not identified leveraging use of your time.

3. You believe that delegation simply means telling people what you want done and expect them to figure out what steps they should take. The result is that most of the tasks delegated do not get done on time and do not meet your standards. Quite often the person might end up spending time on unproductive tasks and might have difficulty meshing with your priorities.

4. You assume that everybody is a self-starter and needs little or no support to complete the required tasks. They might seek you out when needed. This could result in being

frequently interrupted for small tasks.

5. This might result in people being stuck waiting for your approval before taking the next step. This usually leaves people feeling frustrated as they could be more productive if they had the required authority. This, usually, is a sign of micro-management.

6. This happens when you put too much emphasis on results and have a tendency to embarrass people when they do not get the task done properly. The culture is more about punishment in making mistakes rather than supporting and encouraging effort and improvement.

7. You believe "no news is good news" – just the opposite of what is true in management. This is also a sign of a manager who is looking to abdicate his role in supporting the team. Usually this manager "barks orders and leaves." When the task is not done, he goes on a tirade and "barks more orders and leaves." This manager lives in blame mode.

8. You might be weak in upholding the standards and quite often are more interested in being liked than empowering people to get the job done. This also reinforces the belief that it is better to produce than manage producers and staff. You might become paranoid about your ability to manage instead of finding ways to improve your skills.

9. You might be too focused on getting the job done but not focused on what are the motivators for the staff. People might feel burn-out or might feel unappreciated.

10. You might be more focused on you and the company goals than taking better care of the people. You might feel that people are usually not motivated and need to be dragged to the finish line. You might also have people who are not the best fit for their roles. You might not be a good listener and might be failing to bring out the best in your people.

Chapter 17

Right People In The Right Seat

Here is a question we get quite often: I already have a team but would like to know whether they are in the right spot or not. What is my next step?

Usually this question arises because the manager likes the people but is failing to get enough productivity from them. It is obvious that he wants to bring more objectivity to the management process.

Another possible reason is that the manager does not feel that he has trained the people adequately. He feels guilty and might feel that he has not given proper support to the team members and that he should do more to help improve the productivity of the team.

Let us go back to the same process we looked at for hiring an employee. We recommend asking questions like the questionnaire in "Are You Ready To Hire"?

Here are a few simple steps to revisit:

1. Get a detailed organization chart with activities.
2. Define the roles of each team member with detailed job descriptions.

3. Use assessment tools to see what are team members' strengths and weaknesses.
4. Redefine roles if necessary.
5. Make sure you are not too attached to retaining employees who have failed to live up to your standards.
6. Another tool at this point is the manager and employee survey (on the next two pages) to get feedback on the manager's style. It is quite an eye-opening exercise for managers.

We remember an incident where the manager was quite far from the viewpoint of his employees. No wonder he had a tough time motivating and managing his staff.

7. We also recommend the book **"Five Dysfunctions Of A Team: A Leadership Fable"** by Patrick M. Lencioni (Jossey-Bass, 2002), and the survey provided in that book.

The Coaching Manager Skills Assessment (Employee fills this survey)

Directions:
For each statement, please circle one number:
1 = Usually; 2 = Sometimes; 3 = Rarely

Employee's Name:
Company:

	Statement	Circle one
1.	Manager is open to suggestions for change from employees	1 2 3
2.	Manager helps employees stay focused on their tasks	1 2 3
3.	Manager knows and utilizes the strengths of employees	1 2 3

4.	Manager makes himself/herself available for brainstorming sessions	1 2 3
5.	Manager takes time to listen and understand employees' concerns	1 2 3
6.	Manager listens intently rather than telling	1 2 3
7.	Manager recognizes people both for their effort and results	1 2 3
8.	Manager criticizes in private and recognizes in public as soon as possible	1 2 3
9.	Manager knows how people like to be rewarded and does so accordingly	1 2 3
10.	Manager is open, honest and caring in his/her communication	1 2 3
11.	Manager discusses with people what they need [material and equipment, authority] to do their work and helps them get it.	1 2 3
12.	It is easy for the manager to give recognition or praise for good work, and does so often	1 2 3
13.	Manager shows people that he/she cares about them as a person	1 2 3
14.	Manager helps each of the workers to develop their abilities	1 2 3
15.	Manager respects the opinions of the people and they know it	1 2 3
16.	Manager discusses each worker's progress with them often	1 2 3

17.	Manager focuses on results, creating an alignment between the inner drives and motivation of the employee, the demands of their role and the needs of the business.	1 2 3
18.	Manager acts out the belief that the people have huge potential	1 2 3
19.	Manager strives to understand rather than "jumping to conclusions"	1 2 3
20.	Manager offers people constructive feedback rather than judgment	1 2 3
21.	Manager gives permission to experiment and considers risk taking in the interests of learning	1 2 3
22.	Manager co-creates solutions with people instead of trying to have all the answers.	1. 2 3
23.	With their input, manager helps employees set clear goals and expectations	1 2 3
24.	Manager employs a non-directive approach and explores fully situations, options and ways forward	1 2 3
25.	Manager partners with each worker until the goals are achieved.	1 2 3

The Coaching Manager Skills Assessment (Manager fills this survey)

Directions:

For each statement, please circle one number:

1 = Usually; 2 = Sometimes; 3 = Rarely

Manager's Name:

Company:

	Statement	Circle one
1.	I am open to suggestions for change from my employees	1 2 3
2.	I help my employees stay focused on their tasks	1 2 3
3.	I know and utilize the strengths of my employees	1 2 3
4.	I make myself available for brainstorming sessions	1 2 3
5.	I take time to listen and understand my employees' concerns	1 2 3
6.	I listen intently rather than telling	1 2 3
7.	I recognize people both for their effort and results	1 2 3
8.	I criticize in private and recognize in public as soon as possible	1 2 3
9.	I know how people like to be rewarded and do so accordingly	1 2 3
10.	I am open, honest and caring in my communication	1 2 3
11.	I discuss with my people what they need [material and equipment, authority] to do their work and help them get it.	1 2 3

12.	It is easy for me to give recognition or praise for good work, and I do so often	1 2 3
13.	I show my people that I care about them as a person	1 2 3
14.	I help each of my workers to develop their abilities	1 2 3
15.	I respect the opinions of my people and they know it	1 2 3
16.	I discuss each worker's progress with them often	1 2 3
17.	I focus on results, creating an alignment between the inner drives and motivation of the employee, the demands of their role and the needs of the business.	1 2 3
18.	I act out the belief that my people have huge potential	1 2 3
19.	I strive to understand rather than "jumping to conclusions	1 2 3
20.	I offer my people constructive feedback rather than judgment	1 2 3
21.	I give permission to experiment and considered risk taking in the interests of learning	1 2 3
22.	I co-create solutions with my people instead of trying to have all the answers.	1 2 3
23.	With their input, I help employees set clear goals and expectations	1 2 3
24.	I employ a non-directive approach and explore fully situations, options and ways forward	1 2 3
25.	I partner with each worker until the goals are achieved.	1 2 3

Appendix 1:
Behavioral Interview Technique

Sample List of Performance Skills/Behavior with Behavioral Interview Questions and Evaluation Rating System

The behavioral interview technique is used by employers to evaluate a candidate's past experiences and behaviors in order to determine potential for future success.

Step 1: The interviewer identifies desired skills and behaviors appropriate to superior job performance. Look at the job description to find your desired behavior, values, and motivators.

Step 2: The interviewer structures open-ended questions and statements to elicit detailed behavioral responses. Candidate's answers should include the situation/task, action taken by candidate and the result created by candidate.

Step 3: The interviewer can evaluate the answers based on selected criteria using a five-point rating system. See suggested scale on the following pages.

Performance Skill(s)	Behavioral Interview Question	Candidate's Answer (Situation/Task, Action & Result)	Evaluation Rating System 1(less) –5 (most)
FOCUS AND DEDICATION TO THE INDUSTRY:	1. Why did you choose your career? 2. At what point did you make this decision? 3. Specifically, what attracts you to this industry as a career?		
ECHNICAL AND PROFESSIONAL KNOWLEDGE: *Candidate's level of understanding of technical and professional information and the ability to apply technical and professional skills.*	1. Sometimes it's easy to get in "over your head". Describe a situation where you had to request help or assistance on a project or assignment. 2. Give an example of how you applied knowledge from previous coursework to a project in another class.		
TEAMWORK: *Working effectively with others in the organization and outside the formal lines of authority (i.e., peers, other units, senior management, and the like) to accomplish organizational goals and to identify and resolve problems.*	1. Considering the impact of your decisions on others. Describe a situation where others you were working with on a project disagreed with your ideas. What did you do? 2. Considering the impact of your decisions on others. Describe a situation in which you found that your results were not up to your supervisor's expectations. What happened? What action did you take? 3. Considering the impact of your decisions on others, tell about a time when you worked with a colleague who was not completing his share of the work. Who, if anyone, did you tell or talk to about it? Did the manager take any steps to correct your colleague? Did you agree or disagree with the manager's actions?		

ADAPTABILITY: *Maintaining effectiveness in varying environments, tasks and responsibilities, or with various types of people*	1. How was your transition from high school to college? Did you face any particular problems? 2. How was your transition from one career to another career? Did you face any particular problems? 3. How was your transition from company to another company within the same industry? Did you face any particular problems? 4. Tell of some situations in which you have had to adjust quickly to changes over which you had no control. What was the impact of the change on you?		
WORK STANDARDS: *Setting high goals or standards of performance for self, subordinates, others and the organization. Experiencing dissatisfaction with average performance.*	1. Compare and contrast the times when you did work which was above the standard with times your work was below the standard. 2. Describe some times when you were not very satisfied or pleased with your performance. What did you do about it? 3. What are your standards of success in school? What have you done to meet these standards? 4. How have you differed from your professors in evaluating your performance? How did you handle the situation?		
JOB MOTIVATION: *The extent to which activities and responsibilities available in the job overlap with activities and responsibilities that result in personal satisfaction.*	1. Give examples of your experiences at school or in a job that were satisfying. Give examples of your experiences that were dissatisfying. 2. What kind of supervisor do you work best for? Provide examples.		

Performance Skill(s)	Behavioral Interview Question	Candidate's Answer (Situation/Task, Action & Result)	Evaluation Rating System 1(less) –5 (most)
INITIATIVE: *Making active attempts to influence events to achieve goals. Self-starting rather than passively accepting. Taking action to achieve goals beyond what is necessarily called for; originating action.*	1. Describe some projects or ideas (not necessarily your own) that were implemented, or carried out successfully primarily because of your efforts. 2. Describe a situation that required a number of things to be done at the same time. How did you handle it? What was the result? 3. Have you found any ways to make a job easier or more rewarding?		
ABILITY TO LEARN: *Assimilating and applying new job-related information promptly.*	1. What tricks or techniques have you learned to make school or a job easier, or to make yourself more effective? How did you learn that?		
PLANNING AND ORGANIZING: *Establishing a course of action for yourself (and/or others) to accomplish specific goals. Planning proper assignments for personnel and appropriately allocating resources.*	1. How do you determine priorities in scheduling your time? Give examples. 2. Describe a time in school when you had many projects or assignments due at the same time. What steps did you take to get them all done?		

COMMUNICATION: *Clearly expressing ideas in writing-including grammar, organization, and structure*	1. Tell of a time when your active listening skills really paid off for you-maybe a time when other people missed the key idea being expressed. 2. What has been your experience in giving presentations to small or large groups? What has been your most successful experience in speech making?	
CUSTOMER SERVICE ORIENTATION: *Making efforts to listen to and understand the customer (both internal and external), anticipating customer needs and giving high priority to customer satisfaction.*	1. Tell of the most difficult customer service experience that you have ever had to handle-perhaps an angry or irate customer. Be specific and tell what you did and what was the outcome?	
SENSITIVITY: *Acting out of consideration for the feelings and needs of others.*	1. Give an example of when you had to work with someone who was difficult to get along with. Why was this person difficult? How did you handle that person? 2. Describe a situation where you found yourself dealing with someone who didn't like you. How did you handle it?	

Evaluation System for Behavioral Interview Questions

An example of a simple rating system that might be used to evaluate your candidate's behavioral interview questions:

5. MUCH MORE THAN ACCEPTABLE:

Significantly above criteria required for successful job performance

4. MORE THAN ACCEPTABLE:

Generally exceeds criteria relative to quality and quantity of behavior required.

3. ACCEPTABLE:

Meets criteria relative to quality and quantity of behavior required.

2. LESS THAN ACCEPTABLE:

Generally does not meet criteria relative to quality and quantity of behavior required.

1. MUCH LESS THAN ACCEPTABLE:

Significantly below criteria required for successful job performance.

Examples of More Behavioral Interview Questions

1. Describe a situation in which you were able to use persuasion to successfully convince someone to see things your way.
2. Describe a time when you were faced with a stressful situation that demonstrated your coping skills.
3. Give me a specific example of a time when you used good judgment and logic in solving a problem.

4. Give me an example of a time when you set a goal and were able to meet or exceed it.

5. Tell me about a time when you had to use your presentation skills to influence someone's opinion.

6. Give me a specific example of a time when you had to conform to a policy with which you did not agree.

7. Please discuss an important written document you were required to complete.

8. Tell me about a time when you had to go above and beyond the call of duty in order to get a job done.

9. Tell me about a time when you had too many things to do and you were required to prioritize your tasks.

10. Give me an example of a time when you had to make a split second decision.

11. What is your typical way of dealing with conflict? Give me an example.

12. Tell me about a time you were able to successfully deal with another person even when that individual might not have personally liked you (or vice versa).

13. Tell me about a difficult decision you've made in the last year.

14. Give me an example of a time when something you tried to accomplish and failed.

15. Give me an example of when you showed initiative and took the lead.

16. Tell me about a recent situation in which you had to deal with a very upset customer or co-worker.

17. Give me an example of a time when you motivated others.

18. Tell me about a time when you delegated a project effectively.

19. Give me an example of a time when you used your fact-finding skills to solve a problem.

20. Tell me about a time when you missed an obvious solution to a problem.

21. Describe a time when you anticipated potential problems and developed preventive measures.
22. Tell me about a time when you were forced to make an unpopular decision.
23. Please tell me about a time you had to fire a friend.
24. Describe a time when you set your sights too high (or too low).

Appendix 2:
Interview Questions Specific for Administrative Assistant, Receptionist, Marketing Specialist and Salesperson

Interview Questions for Marketing Position

1. What is **marketing**?
2. Tell us about a marketing plan that you have developed and the result of implementing that plan.
3. What is a **marketing plan**?
4. What should a marketing plan address?
5. What is a **market niche**?
6. Which environmental variables impact a marketing plan?
7. What are **demographics**?
8. Which marketing research tools and techniques have you used?
9. Tell us about a marketing questionnaire that you have developed. What did you learn from the questionnaire?

Interview Questions for Sales Position

1. What steps do you take to overcome a prospect's sales resistance?
2. What techniques do you use to handle objections?
3. What techniques do you use to handle procrastination?
4. Tell us about your closing technique.
5. What are some of the ways you create a sense of urgency to close the sale?
6. How do you handle a customer with buyer's remorse?
7. Tell me about the most difficult sale you have made. What did you learn from it?
8. Tell me about the largest sale that you have lost.

Interview Questions for Receptionist

1. What are some of the techniques that you can use to make a visitor feel more comfortable?
2. How would you greet a visitor to the office?
3. You have a number of people in the office waiting for help. How will you handle the people?
4. What experience have you had as a <u>receptionist</u>?

Public contact and customer service experience can supplement or substitute for receptionist experience.

Interview Questions for Administrative Assistant Position

1. Tell us about your proofreading experience.
2. What experience have you had in maintaining a manager's work schedule?
3. What do you consider before committing your manager to a meeting?
4. What are the three major types of errors that should be considered when proofreading a document?
5. What reference sources should you use to ensure that an outgoing correspondence is accurate and correct?
6. What are the basic components of a business letter?
7. Tell us about your experience as an administrative assistant.

Don't forget to mention how many managers you supported or their level.

8. Under which circumstances would you use a memorandum instead of a letter?

Usually memorandums are for internal communications while letters are used for external communications.

9. What experience have you had in <u>typing letters</u>?
10. What experience have you had in <u>typing reports</u>?
11. What experience have you had in <u>typing data tables</u>?
12. What experience have you had in typing newsletter?
13. What experience do you have with mail merge and organizing data for a mailing house?
14. Name the most common forms of punctuation and describe their use.

Appendix 3:
Candidate Interview Checklist

Elements of the Interview Process	Criteria	Interviewer's Comments
Resume	• Adequate Experience • No large gaps in chronology (job hopping) • Neat and well-written • No typographical or grammatical errors	
Cover Letter	• Able to summarize how it is a good job fit. • Neat and well-written • No typographical or grammatical errors	
Phone	• Gave thoughtful, succinct answers. • Pleasant phone voice. • Pleasant demeanor.	
Written Interview	• Legible handwriting • Gave well-written, thoughtful, succinct answers	
Face-to-Face Interview	General Impressions: • Professional appearance • Gave eye contact and smile • Good non-verbal communication • Used proper professional vocabulary • Used voice and volume in professional manner • Handshake • Answered all questions • Asked interviewer questions	

Elements of the Interview Process	Criteria	Interviewer's Comments
Assessments	• DISC • Motivators • Axiology-based tool • Fear of prospecting • Others	
Thank You Note or Email	• Received in timely manner • Summarizes the interview • Candidate is able to articulate contribution to the organization	

Thank you so much for the help today. I cannot believe how accurate those tests were in comparison to how my employees styles are. The reports were right on!

I can't wait to share this concept of screening employees and learning how to manage them better with everyone. Our conversation could not have come at a better time. You have me fired up!

—Rene Nelson, Loan Officer, OR

Minesh Baxi's assessments are nothing short of amazing. Before hiring new members for my business team I had myself tested. It was rather revealing to see how I was assessed. I was reassured of the strengths that I knew I had, but I was surprised by my extremely weak aspects of my personality. I was given a road map for self-improvement. Once I was tested I realized that I had all the wrong people working on my personal loan production team. I let everyone go and started over. I worked a lot of hours for that month! Using Minesh's guidance, I interviewed new people for my team. I had the one I liked best tested, and to my delight, she was a great match. Most importantly, I was given direction by Minesh's on how to best manage her. As an added bonus, she is personally more productive than the two people that she replaced combined! Thank you Minesh!

—Mike Burwell, Director of Sales,
Pacific Blue Equity, CA

Hiring my first employee was a huge step and having Minesh and Kim in my corner made all the difference. Their assessment of my personality was dead on and after working with my assistant for the past three quarters, their assessment of her was dead on as well, everything from her strengths to her weaknesses. Great resource, don't hire without their input!

—Matthew I. Snowden, Loan Officer, AZ

Minesh Baxi 's interpretation on my DISC/Behavior Assessment helped me realize what was preventing me from being an effective communicator. I highly recommend taking these assessments to get a better understanding of your communication style and also to dramatically improve your communication with your team and other people in your life.

—Tony Tylman, Loan Officer, TX

Claim Your FREE
"Get More Done With Less" Manager's Kit

You will receive:

1. "How Are You In Delegating" Survey
2. FREE 25-minute complimentary management audit session to create action plan based on your report

Email minesh@mbaxi.com or call 248-866-0063
or visit www.StopHiringLosers.com to get your FREE kit.

Name: _____

Company: _____

Title/Role: _____

Email Address: _____

Address: _____

City/State: _____

Zip Code: _____

Phone Number: _____

Made in the USA
San Bernardino, CA
18 August 2017